MW01634044

ALIVE TO

Wonder

Celebrating the Influence of C.S. Lewis

JOHN PIPER

Published by Desiring God
Post Office Box 2901
Minneapolis, MN 55402
www.desiringGod.org

Cover design and typesetting
Taylor Design Works

TABLE OF CONTENTS

INTRODUCTION

C.S. Lewis died fifty years ago this year. "More than a generation after his death, Lewis's works are now more popular and widely read than at any point during his lifetime."[1] His thought is so creative and so profound and so extensive that Alister McGrath says, "Half a century after his death, the process of receiving and interpreting Lewis has still only begun."[2]

I put Lewis in the top three writers who have influenced how I read and respond to the world. Yes, the world is a book to be read. And few people could read like Lewis. When Clyde Kilby wrote an anthology of Lewis's writings he titled it *A Mind Awake*. He might have called it "An Awakening Mind." This is the effect it has. His alertness to reality is contagious.

My tribute to Lewis is scattered all through my writings and sermons. I want to thank Jonathan Parnell for gathering together all the parts of this book and providing the editorial sutures that transform them into a readable flow. This is our celebration of Lewis's extraordinary gift of being *Awake to Wonder.*

The Magisterial Humility of C.S. Lewis

One way to appreciate C.S. Lewis is to see how his Christian humility shaped his life and work. Owen Barfield, one of Lewis's closest friends, said that the "new voice" with which he spoke after his conversion had an "unmistakable note of magisterial humility."[3]

What does "magisterial humility" look like? That is what this introduction is about.

Self-Forgetfulness

I first met Lewis's humility embodied in one of his foremost American advocates in the 1960s, Clyde Kilby. Dr. Kilby taught English Literature at Wheaton College for 46 years. He carried on a personal correspondence with Lewis from 1943 until Lewis died in 1963. This correspondence became the seed for the personal papers of the Lewis circle (the Inklings) which Kilby gathered in the founding of the Marion E. Wade Center at Wheaton College.

Kilby was utterly disinterested in himself, and was full of love for God and his stunning gifts in the world of nature and literature. This was Kilby's gift to people—his love for them. He would come into class, open his Bible, and begin to read Job 39,

> Is it by your understanding that the hawk soars
>   and spreads his wings toward the south?
> Is it at your command that the eagle mounts up
>   and makes his nest on high? (Job 39:26–27)

His smile would burst into laughter. And his eyes would sparkle and when he looked up at us his countenance would say, "Have you seen this? Did you know this? Isn't this amazing? Do you have eyes for this?" Then he would turn to John Keats and read "To Autumn,"

> Season of mists and mellow fruitfulness
> Close bosom-friend of the maturing sun
> Conspiring with him how to load and bless
> With fruit the vines that round the thatch-eaves
> run...

And he would say, "If you memorize this, it will bring you great pleasure when you are old." I don't think I ever heard Clyde Kilby make a comment about the subjective states of Clyde Kilby. He was a wonderfully healthy incarnation of self-forgetfulness.

Years later, Dr. Kilby came to Minneapolis and gave a self-reflective list of steps to mental health. But, as expected, the list included:

> I shall not demean my own uniqueness by envy of others. I shall stop boring into myself to discover what psychological or social categories I might belong to. Mostly I shall simply forget about myself and do my work.[4]

This healthy, humble gift of self-forgetfulness Dr. Kilby shared with C.S. Lewis. There is so much greatness to be known and felt by looking at God and his world, they believed, why would we focus on ourselves? Walter Hooper, Lewis's secretary, said,

Although Lewis owned a huge library, he possessed few of his own works. His phenomenal memory recorded almost everything he had read except his own writings—an appealing fault. Often when I quoted lines from his own poems he would ask who the author was. He was a very great scholar, but no expert in the field of C.S. Lewis.[5]

The Real Business of Life

In diminishing his own preoccupation with himself, Lewis's humility enabled him to see what was really valuable, even when it was not his own literary vocation. How many prominent literary men are willing to speak the truth that Lewis spoke so plainly?

> The Christian knows from the outset that the salvation of a single soul is more important than the production or preservation of all the epics and tragedies in the world: and as for superiority, he knows that the vulgar since they include most of the poor probably include most of his superiors.[6]

Lewis had no time for those who called literature an end in itself, or thought that literature existed "for its own sake."

> It is hard not to argue that all the greatest poems have been made by men who valued something else much more than poetry—even if that something else were only cutting down enemies in a cattle-raid or tumbling a girl in bed. The real frivolity, the solemn vacuity, is all with those who make

literature a self-existent thing to be valued for its
own sake.[7]

Nothing but God exists "for its own sake." Lewis's humility prevents him from defending his own turf as he tackles the question, "What is the value of culture?" He knows what the answer is not: "No one, presumably, is really maintaining that a fine taste in the arts is a condition of salvation. Yet the glory of God, and, as our only means to glorifying him, the salvation of human souls, is the real business of life."[8]

His humility inclines him to speak in tune with ultimate authority, the Bible: "I think we can still believe culture to be innocent after reading the New Testament; I cannot see that we are encouraged to think it is important."[9] Yet, he says, it is important. It has a modest place in life:

> I conclude that culture has a distinct part to play
> in bringing certain souls to Christ. Not all souls—
> there is a shorter, and safer way which has always
> been followed by thousands of simple affectional
> natures who begin, where we hope to end, with
> devotion to the person of Christ.[10]

Keep in mind, these are words coming from a man whom even his critics said "was the best read man of his generation, one who read everything and remembered everything he read."[11] His was "magisterial humility." His eyes had been opened to see what is really valuable in the world and how his little sphere of literature, glorious as it is, humbly fits in: "The work of a charwoman and the work of a poet become spiritual in the same way and on the same condition."[12]

Simply Being

Behind these expressions of humility lay a very simple, powerful, basic humility concerning being—the humility that admits, submits to, and rejoices in the fact that things exists outside oneself. To put it another way, Lewis's humility inclined him to believe he was not the measure of all things, but that objective and ultimate reality existed outside him, and did not depend on him for their existence or meaning.

Ultimate relativism, nihilism, and post-modernism are all forms of pride. If there is no objective reality outside of me, then I don't have to submit to it. Lewis thought that such views would mean the "abolition of man." In a book by that title he defended "the doctrine of objective value, the belief that certain attitudes are really true, and others really false to the kind of thing the universe is and the kind of things we are."[13] So Lewis devoted his life not to creating reality, but to seeing it and saying it well.

> An author should never conceive himself as
> bringing into existence beauty or wisdom which
> did not exist before, but simply and solely as trying
> to embody in terms of his own art some reflection
> of eternal Beauty and Wisdom.[14]

That is the response of humility to the world one is given by a Creator. It inclines one to love truth and to endeavor for all one's ideas to fit the truth. Hence Clyde Kilby said of Lewis, "He liked his ideas to fit the truth as snugly as old slippers fit the feet."[15] Pride does not care about this fit. Pride wants other things to fit with it. Not the reverse. Humility submits to God's willed reality and makes the effort to conform its ideas to Truth.

The Sovereignty of God

As we would expect, therefore, Lewis's humility submitted to the sovereignty of God. Part of the objective reality outside himself to which Lewis submitted was the purposefulness of God. "You will certainly carry out God's purposes, however you act, but it makes a difference to you whether you serve like Judas or like John."[16]

> Where a God who is totally purposive and totally foreseeing acts upon a Nature which is totally interlocked, there can be no accidents or loose ends, nothing whatever of which we can safely use the word *merely*. Nothing is 'merely a by-product' of anything else. All results are intended from the first.[17]

Or as Puddleglum said in *The Silver Chair*, "Don't you mind him. There are no accidents. Our guide is Aslan."[18] The explicit biblical ground for calling this a form of humility is James 4:15–16. "Instead you ought to say, 'If the Lord wills, we will live and do this or that.' As it is, you boast in your *arrogance*. All such boasting is evil." It is arrogant not to recognize and affirm that staying alive and doing anything is owing to the sovereign will of God. Lewis did not make this mistake.

The Source of Meaning

Lewis's humility disinclined him from making his understanding of a writing the definition of its meaning. Rather he was inclined to seek the author's intention. This is a particular application of his belief that there is reality outside himself and that he is not the measure of all things. The intentions of authors are part of that reality. His defense of this view is disarming in its humility:

> The literary scholars ... ask, "Why should I turn from a real and present experience—what the poem means to me, what happens to me when I read it—to inquiries about the poet's intention or reconstructions ...?" There seem to be two answers. One is that the poem in my head which I make from my mistranslations of Chaucer or misunderstandings of Donne may possibly not be so good as the work Chaucer or Donne actually made.
>
> Secondly, why not have both? After enjoying what I made of it, why not go back to the text, this time looking up the hard words, puzzling out the illusions, and discovering that some metrical delights in my first experience were due to my fortunate mispronunciations, and see whether I can enjoy the poet's poem, not necessarily instead of, but in addition to, my own one?[19]

It is humble to admit that the poem the author actually wrote might be better than the one you create out of your own head by using the raw verbal symbols that the author happened to supply for you on the page.

Actually, I think Lewis was perhaps being too easy on the subjectivists, since his Christian faith also commends the Golden Rule, which in this case would mean: Do unto authors as you would have them do unto you. And most of us write to communicate something, rather than simply to throw things on the page for others to make of them what they will.

Since God is real outside ourselves and has sent us a book, his intention in what the book says is of infinite importance. How to read the Bible is a good example of how to read everything—humbly, as though we have something to see—something to learn—from another mind.

Friendship

Humility inclined Lewis not just to learn "from" another mind, but "with" another mind. What I am thinking of here is his experience of, and writing about, friendship. Friendship is two or more people engaging in a kind of corporate self-forgetfulness. Their focus is on something outside the group. Here's how Lewis put it:

> In some ways nothing is less like a friendship than
> a love-affair. Lovers are always talking to one
> another about their love; friends hardly ever about
> their friendship. Lovers are normally face-to-
> face, absorbed in each other; friends, side-by-side,
> absorbed in some common interest. ... In this kind
> of love, as Emerson said, *"Do you love me?"* means
> *"Do you see the same truth?"*—Or at least, "Do you

care about the same truth?" The man who agrees with us that some question, little regarded by others, is of great importance, can be our friend. He need not agree with us about the answer.[20]

This has affected my view of friendship ever since I read it. I love the camaraderie of common passions focused on some great object outside ourselves.

Our Spiritual Condition

Finally, Lewis's humility opened his mind to see the difference between gift-love and need-love in the way God loves us and we love God. Humility is happy to discover that the greatness of God consigns us forever to the position of needy in relation to him. We don't work for him. He works for us.

"God is not served by human hands as though he needed anything" (Acts 17:25). "The Son of Man came not to be served" (Mark 10:45). If God were hungry he would not tell us, for the cattle on a thousand hills are his (Ps. 50:9–15). "God works for those who wait for him" (Isa. 64:4). We are the needy. God is forever the Provider, Protector, Treasure.

> Need-love ... makes a main ingredient in man's highest, healthiest, and most realistic spiritual condition. A very strange corollary follows. Man approaches God most nearly when he is in one sense least like God. For what can be more unlike than fullness and need, sovereignty and humility, righteousness and penitence, limitless power and

a cry for help? This paradox staggered me when I first ran into it; it also wrecked all my previous attempts to write about love.[21]

Profound Thankfulness

In the first chapter of this book I will express my misgivings about C.S. Lewis's views on some important doctrines. It may be dismaying to some that I would value so highly a man with whom I would disagree on so many things. To others it may be dismaying that I would even point out the doctrinal flaws of American evangelicalism's patron saint.[22] But the point of doing it is to underline the need for Lewis's kind of humility.

This "magisterial humility" did not keep him from all error. But it kept him from some of the worst errors of his age—and our age. Our humility will no doubt not keep us from all errors. But if we learn from Lewis what we can—and this is immeasurable—we will embrace truth more wisely and more humbly, even the truth he didn't see.

In this fiftieth year since he died, I offer this little book as a celebration of the influence of C.S. Lewis in my life. I hope I do so in humility. I know I do so with profound thankfulness.

THE IRONIC EFFECT: DEEPENED UNSHARED CONVICTIONS

From "Lessons from an Inconsolable Soul: Learning from the Mind and Heart of C.S. Lewis," February 2, 2010

My approach in this first chapter is personal. I am going to talk about what has meant the most to me in C.S. Lewis—how he has helped me the most. As I raise this question, as I have many times over the years, the backdrop of the question becomes increasingly urgent. Why has C.S. Lewis been so significant for me, even though he is not Reformed in his doctrine, and could barely be called an evangelical by typical American use of that word?

Lewis did not believe in the inerrancy of Scripture,[23] and he defaulted to logical arguments more naturally than to biblical exegesis. He did not treat the Reformation with respect, but thought it could have been avoided, and called aspects of it farcical.[24] He steadfastly refused in public or in letters to explain why he was not a Roman Catholic but remained in the Church of England.[25] He made room for at least some people to be saved through imperfect representations of Christ in other religions.[26] He made a strong logical, but I think unbiblical, case for free will to explain why there is suffering in the world.[27] He spoke of the atonement with reverence, but put little significance on any of the explanations for how it actually saves sinners.[28]

In other words, Lewis is not a writer to whom we should turn for growth in a careful biblical understanding of Christian doctrine. There is almost no passage of Scripture on which I would turn to Lewis for exegetical illumination — there are a few, but not many. He did not deal with many. If we follow him in the kinds of mistakes that he made (the ones listed above), it will hurt the church and dishonor Christ. His value is not in his biblical exegesis. Lewis is not the kind of writer who provides substance for a pastor's sermons. If a pastor treats Lewis as a resource for doctrinal substance, he will find his messages growing thin, perhaps interesting, but not with much rich biblical content.

So you see the kind of backdrop there is for this ebook. How and why has C.S. Lewis been so helpful to me when I think he is so wrong on some very important matters? Why don't I put Lewis in the same category as the so-called "emergent" writers? At one level, the mistakes seem similar. But when I pose the question that way, it starts to become pretty clear to me why Lewis keeps being useful, while I think the emergent voices have faded away fairly quickly.

In fact, I think posing the question this way not only explains why he has been so helpful to me, but also goes right to the heart of what the life and work of C.S. Lewis were about. There was something at the core of his work—of his mind—that had the ironic effect on me of awakening lively affections and firm convictions that he himself would not have held.

There was something about the way Lewis read Scripture that made my own embrace of inerrancy tighter, not looser. There was something about the way he spoke of grace and God's power that made me value the particularities of the Reformation more, not less. There was something about the way he portrayed the wonders of the incarnation that made me more suspicious of his own inclusivism, not less. There was something about the way he spoke of doctrine as the necessary roadmap that leads to Reality,29 and the way he esteemed truth and reason and precision of thought, that made me cherish more, not less, the historic articulations of the biblical explanations of how the work of Christ saves sinners—the so-called theories of the atonement.

It may be that others, by Lewis, have been drawn away from these kinds of convictions and experiences. But I doubt very seriously that more people on the whole have been weakened in true biblical commitments than have been strengthened by reading Lewis.

THE SYNTHESIS:
WHEN MIND MET HEART

From "Pastor As Scholar: A Personal Journey," April 23, 2009

My love of reading and writing led me to be a literature major in college. The literature faculty at Wheaton College was renowned. I tried to take every poetry class that was offered. And I avoided every novel class that was offered. I could not read fast enough to get through the novels in a semester, but I could write and analyze poetry. So I carefully navigated my way through a literature major as one of the slowest readers on campus.

Mainly, though, the poetry was chosen because the emotions of a young man can run deep in the river of poetry. Clyde Kilby was a giant in the literature department in those days, and his book *Poetry and Life* was lived out in front of us in class. Kilby took the passion for observation and breathed a kind of life into it that biology never could. He taught me there is always more to see in what I see. There is always wonder. There is always something to be astonished about. There is mental health in learning to look at a tree or a cloud or a nose and marvel that it is what it is. This then became poetry. When you finally see the wonder of what you have been looking at for 10 years, what you do with that seeing is try to say it, and that is what poetry is. When what you see is God, there is only a fine line between poetry and preaching.

One of Kilby's resolutions for being a healthy person read like this: "I shall open my eyes and ears. Once every day, I shall simply stare at a tree, a flower, a cloud, or a person. I shall not then be concerned at all to ask *what* they are, but simply be glad *that* they are. I shall joyfully allow them the mystery of, what Lewis calls, 'their divine, magical, terrifying, and ecstatic existence.'"

When you are being helped to see what you've always looked at all your life and never seen, it is absolutely revolutionary. Kilby was one of the greatest influences of my life, and I scarcely know what he thought about anything. It was the way he saw the world and spoke of the world. He was so alive to the wonder of things. This was incalculably valuable preparation of soul for the vision of God that would come in just a few years at seminary.

Most of this section in my life belongs to Noël Henry. She has been my wife for over four decades. But in those days, starting in the summer of 1966, she was this ravishing object of desire. Oh, how I wanted to be married to Noël! Falling in love is very powerful. Not in vain does the Song of Solomon say, "I adjure you, O daughters of Jerusalem, that you not stir up or awaken love until it pleases" (Song 8:4). The effects of finding a wife are so pervasive and long-lasting that they are immeasurable. Here is where Noël entered my life and nothing has been the same since. I owe her more than anyone else in the world.

The synthesis of mind and heart was embodied in C.S. Lewis. Lewis became for me in my college days what Jonathan Edwards became in my seminary days. He was a "romantic rationalist"—that was the name of a small book about Lewis that got me very excited because it summed up what I thought I was (which may be very akin to "pastor-scholar"). Lewis has had a tremendous influence on me in several ways.

Lewis embodied the fact that rigorous, precise, penetrating logic is not inimical to deep, soul-stirring feeling and vivid, lively—even playful—imagination. He combined what almost everybody today assumes are mutually exclusive terms: rationalism and poetry, cool logic and warm feeling, disciplined prose and free imagination. In shattering these old stereotypes, he freed me to think hard and to write poetry, to argue for the resurrection and to compose hymns to Christ, to smash an argument and to hug a friend, to demand a definition and to use a metaphor.

Lewis was the main influence on Clyde Kilby. And so Lewis had the same effect on me. He gave me an intense sense of the "realness" of things: to wake up in the morning and be aware of the firmness of the mattress, the warmth of the sun rays, the sound of the clock ticking, the sheer being of things ("quiddity" as he calls it). He helped me become alive to life. He helped me see what is there in the world—things which if we didn't have, we would pay a million dollars to have, but having them, we ignore.

Finally, he has made me wary of chronological snobbery.

That is, he has shown me that "newness" is no virtue, and "oldness" is no fault. Truth and beauty and goodness are not determined by *when* they exist. Nothing is inferior for being old, and nothing is valuable for being modern. This has freed me from the tyranny of novelty.

These lessons were immeasurable gifts and had the effect of synthesizing my college experience. The intellectual stimulation, the emotional deepening, the stirring of imagination, the passion to write—all of these came together in C.S. Lewis.

THE PROBLEM: TOO EASILY PLEASED

From Desiring God: Meditations of a Christian Hedonist, *Revised edition, (Colorado Springs: Multnomah, 2011), 19–20*

I grew to love the works of C.S. Lewis in college. But not until later did I buy his sermon called "The Weight of Glory." The first page of that sermon is one of the most influential pages of literature I have ever read. It goes like this:

> If you asked twenty good men today what they thought the highest of the virtues, nineteen of them would reply, Unselfishness. But if you asked almost any of the great Christians of old he would have replied, Love. You see what has happened? A negative term has been substituted for a positive, and this is of more than philological importance. The negative ideal of Unselfishness

carries with it the suggestion not primarily of securing good things for others, but of going without them ourselves, as if our abstinence and not their happiness was the important point. I do not think this is the Christian virtue of Love. The New Testament has lots to say about self-denial, but not about self-denial as an end in itself. We are told to deny ourselves and to take up our crosses in order that we may follow Christ; and nearly every description of what we shall ultimately find if we do so contains an appeal to desire.

If there lurks in most modern minds the notion that to desire our own good and earnestly to hope for the enjoyment of it is a bad thing, I submit that this notion has crept in from Kant and the Stoics and is no part of the Christian faith. Indeed, if we consider the unblushing promises of reward and the staggering nature of the rewards promised in the Gospels, it would seem that Our Lord finds our desires not too strong, but too weak. We are half-hearted creatures, fooling about with drink and sex and ambition when infinite joy is offered us, like an ignorant child who wants to go on making mud pies in a slum because he cannot imagine what is meant by the offer of a holiday at the sea. We are far too easily pleased.[30]

There it was in black and white, and to my mind it was totally compelling: It is not a bad thing to desire our own good. In fact, the great problem of human beings is that they are far too easily pleased. They don't seek pleasure with nearly the resolve and passion that they should. And so they settle for mud pies of appetite instead of infinite delight.

I had never in my whole life heard any Christian, let alone a Christian of Lewis's stature, say that all of us not only seek (as Pascal said), but also ought to seek, our own happiness. Our mistake lies not in the intensity of our desire for happiness, but in the weakness of it.

Another insight was there in Lewis's sermon, but Pascal made it more explicit. He goes on to say:

> There once was in man a true happiness of which now remain to him only the mark and empty trace, which he in vain tries to fill from all his surroundings, seeking from things absent the help he does not obtain in things present. But these are all inadequate, because the infinite abyss can only be filled by an infinite and immutable object, that is to say, only by God Himself.[31]

As I look back on it now, it seems so patently obvious that I don't know how I could have missed it. All those years I had been trying to suppress my tremendous longing for happiness so I could honestly praise God out of some "higher," less selfish motive. But now it started to dawn on me that this persistent and undeniable yearning for happiness was not to be suppressed, but to be glutted— on God! The growing conviction that praise should be motivated solely by the happiness we find in God seemed less and less strange.

The next insight came again from C.S. Lewis, but this time from his *Reflections on the Psalms.* Chapter 9 of

Lewis's book bears the modest title "A Word about Praise." In my experience it has been *the* word about praise—the best word on the nature of praise I have ever read.

Lewis says that as he was beginning to believe in God, a great stumbling block was the presence of demands scattered through the Psalms that he should praise God. He did not see the point in all this; besides, it seemed to picture God as craving "for our worship like a vain woman who wants compliments." He goes on to show why he was wrong:

> But the most obvious fact about praise—whether of God or anything—strangely escaped me. I thought of it in terms of compliment, approval, or the giving of honor. I had never noticed that all enjoyment spontaneously overflows into praise.... The world rings with praise—lovers praising their mistresses, readers their favorite poet, walkers praising the countryside, players praising their favorite game ...
>
> My whole, more general difficulty about the praise of God depended on my absurdly denying to us, as regards the supremely Valuable, what we delight to do, what indeed we can't help doing, about everything else we value.
>
> I think we delight to praise what we enjoy because the praise not merely expresses but completes the enjoyment; it is its appointed consummation.[32]

This was the capstone of my emerging Hedonism. Praising God, the highest calling of humanity and our eternal vocation, did not involve the renunciation, but rather the consummation of the joy I so desired. My old effort to achieve worship with no self-interest in it proved to be a contradiction in terms. God is not worshiped where He is not treasured and enjoyed. Praise is not an alternative to joy, but the expression of joy. Not to enjoy God is to dishonor Him. To say to Him that something else satisfies you more is the opposite of worship. It is sacrilege.

THE OLD IDEA: CHRISTIAN HEDONISM FROM THE GREATS

From When I Don't Desire God: How to Fight for Joy, *(Wheaton: Crossway, 2011), 15–19*

I want to help those who are starting to see that conversion is the creation of new desires, not just new duties; new delights, not just new deeds; new treasures, not just new tasks.

Far and wide people are seeing these truths in the Bible. They are discovering that there is nothing new about Christian Hedonism at all, but that it is simple, old-fashioned, historic, biblical, radical Christian living. It is as old as the psalmists who said to God, "Restore to me the joy of your salvation" (Ps. 51:12) and "Satisfy us in the morning with your steadfast love" (Ps. 90:14).

It's as old as Jesus, who gave to his people this virtually impossible command for the day of their persecution: "Rejoice in that day, and leap for joy, for behold, your reward is great in heaven" (Luke 6:23).

It's as old as the early Christians, who "*joyfully* accepted the plundering of [their] property," because they "had a better possession and an abiding one" (Heb. 10:34).

It's as old as Augustine, who described conversion as the triumph of sovereign joy:

> How sweet all at once it was for me to be rid of those fruitless joys which I had once feared to lose … ! You drove them from me, you who are the true, the sovereign joy. You drove them from me and took their place, you who are sweeter than all pleasure, though not to flesh and blood, you who outshine all light, yet are hidden deeper than any secret in our hearts, you who surpass all honor, though not in the eyes of men who see all honor in themselves. … O Lord my God, my Light, my Wealth, and my Salvation.[33]

It's as old as John Calvin, the great Reformer of Geneva, who said in his 1559 *Institutes of the Christian Religion* that aspiring after happiness in union with God is "the chief activity of the soul."

> If human happiness, whose perfection it is to be united with God, were hidden from man, he would in fact be bereft of the principal use of his understanding. Thus, also the chief activity of the soul is to aspire thither. Hence the more anyone endeavors to approach to God, the more he proves himself endowed with reason.[34]

It's as old as the Puritans, like Thomas Watson, who wrote in 1692 that God counts himself more glorified when we find more happiness in his salvation:

> Would it not be an encouragement to a subject, to
> hear his prince say to him, "You will honor and
> please me very much, if you will go to yonder mine
> of gold, and dig as much gold for yourself as you
> can carry away?" So, for God to say, "Go to the
> ordinances, get as much grace as you can, dig out as
> much salvation as you can; and the more happiness
> you have, the more I shall count myself glorified."[35]

It's as old as Jonathan Edwards, who argued with all his intellectual might in 1729 that "persons need not and ought not to set any bounds to their spiritual and gracious appetites." Rather, they ought

> to be endeavoring by all possible ways to inflame
> their desires and to obtain more spiritual pleasures.
> ... Our hungerings and thirstings after God and
> Jesus Christ and after holiness can't be too great
> for the value of these things, for they are things of
> infinite value. ... [Therefore] endeavor to promote
> spiritual appetites by laying yourself in the way of
> allurement ... .[36] There is no such thing as excess in
> our taking of this spiritual food. There is no such
> virtue as temperance in spiritual feasting.[37]

It's as old as Princeton theologian Charles Hodge, who argued in the nineteenth century that the true knowledge of Christ includes (and does not just lead to) delight in Christ. This knowledge "is not the apprehension of what he is, simply by the intellect, but also ... involves not as its consequence merely, but as one of its elements, the corresponding feeling of adoration, *delight, desire and complacency* [contentment]."[38]

It is as old as the Reformed New Testament scholar Geerhardus Vos, who in the early twentieth century conceded that there is in the writings of the apostle Paul "a spiritualized type of hedonism."

> Of course, it is not intended to deny to Paul that transfigured *spiritualized type of "hedonism"* if one prefers so to call it, as distinct from the specific attitude towards life that went in the later Greek philosophy by that technical name. Nothing, not even a most refined Christian experience and cultivation of religion are possible without that. … Augustine speaks of this in his *Confessions* in these words: "*For there exists a delight* that is not given to the wicked, but to those honoring Thee, O God, without desiring recompense, the joy of whom Thou art Thyself! And this is the blessed life, to rejoice towards Thee, about Thee, for Thy sake." (Conf. X, 32)[39]

It's as old as the great C.S. Lewis, who died the same day as John F. Kennedy and had a huge influence on the way I experience nature worshipfully.

> Pleasures are shafts of glory as it strikes our sensibility. … But aren't there bad, unlawful pleasures? Certainly there are. But in calling them "bad pleasures" I take it we are using a kind of shorthand. We mean "pleasures snatched by unlawful acts." It is the stealing of the apples that

is bad, not the sweetness. The sweetness is still
a beam from the glory. ... I have tried since ... to
make every pleasure into a channel of adoration.
I don't mean simply by giving thanks for it. One
must of course give thanks, but I meant something
different ... Gratitude exclaims, very properly,
"How good of God to give me this." Adoration says,
"What must be the quality of that Being whose
far-off and momentary coruscations are like this!"
One's mind runs back up the sunbeam to the sun.
... If this is *Hedonism*, it is also a somewhat arduous
discipline. But it is worth some labour.[40]

Lewis was so influential in my understanding of joy and desire and duty and worship that I will add another quotation from him as a tribute to the greatness of his wisdom. I hope my enthusiasm for Lewis will set you to reading him, if you haven't. He, of course, had his flaws, but few people in the twentieth century had eyes to see what he saw. For example, few saw, as he did, the proper place of duty and delight:

Provided the thing is in itself right, the more one
likes it and the less one has to "try to be good," the
better. A *perfect* man would never act from sense of
duty; he'd always *want* the right thing more than
the wrong one. Duty is only a substitute for love
(of God and of other people), like a crutch, which
is a substitute for a leg. Most of us need the crutch
at times; but of course it's idiotic to use the crutch
when our own legs (our own loves, tastes, habits,
etc.) can do the journey on their own![41]

The point of citing all these witnesses is that lots of people, with good reason, are being persuaded that Christian Hedonism is simple, old-fashioned, historic, biblical, radical Christian living, not some new spiritual technique. They are discovering that *God is most glorified in us when we are most satisfied in him.* Which means they are finding that their desires, not just their decisions, really matter. The glory of God is at stake.

THE HIGHEST VIRTUE:
WHY GOD SEEKS HIS OWN GLORY

From Desiring God: Meditations of a Christian Hedonist, *Revised edition, (Colorado Springs: Multnomah, 2011), 48–50.*

Consider this question: In view of God's infinite power and wisdom and beauty, what would his love for a human being involve? Or to put it another way: What could God give us to enjoy that would prove him most loving? There is only one possible answer: himself! If he withholds himself from our contemplation and companionship, no matter what else he gives us, he is not loving.

Now we are on the brink of what for me was a life-changing discovery. What do we all do when we are given or shown something beautiful or excellent? We praise it! We praise new little babies: "Oh, look at that nice round head, and all that hair! And her hands: aren't they perfect?" We praise a lover after a long absence: "Your eyes are like a cloudless sky! Your hair is like forest silk!" We

praise a grand slam in the bottom of the ninth when we
are down by three. We praise the October trees along the
banks of the St. Croix.

But the great discovery for me, as I said, came while
I was reading "A Word about Praise" in C.S. Lewis's
Reflections on the Psalms. His recorded thoughts—born
from wrestling with the idea that God not only wants our
praise, but commands it—bear looking at again, in fuller
form:

> But the most obvious fact about praise—whether
> of God or any thing—strangely escaped me. I
> thought of it in terms of compliment, approval, or
> the giving of honor. I had never noticed that all
> enjoyment spontaneously overflows into praise
> unless (sometimes even if) shyness or the fear of
> boring others is deliberately brought in to check
> it. The world rings with praise—lovers praising
> their mistresses, readers their favorite poet,
> walkers praising the countryside, players praising
> their favorite game—praise of weather, wines,
> dishes, actors, motors, horses, colleges, countries,
> historical personages, children, flowers, mountains,
> rare stamps, rare beetles, even sometimes
> politicians or scholars. I had not noticed how the
> humblest, and at the same time most balanced and
> capacious, minds praised most, while the cranks,
> misfits and mal-contents praised least. ...
>
> I had not noticed either that just as men
> spontaneously praise whatever they value, so they
> spontaneously urge us to join them in praising

it: "Isn't she lovely? Wasn't it glorious? Don't you think that magnificent?" The Psalmists in telling everyone to praise God are doing what all men do when they speak of what they care about. My whole, more general, difficulty about the praise of God depended on my absurdly denying to us, as regards the supremely Valuable, what we delight to do, what indeed we can't help doing, about everything else we value.

I think we delight to praise what we enjoy because the praise not merely expresses but completes the enjoyment; it is its appointed consummation. It is not out of compliment that lovers keep on telling one another how beautiful they are; the delight is incomplete till it is expressed.[42]

There is the solution! We praise what we enjoy because the delight is incomplete until it is expressed in praise. If we were not allowed to speak of what we value, and celebrate what we love, and praise what we admire, our joy would not be full. So if God loves us enough to make our joy full, he must not only give us himself; he must also win from us the praise of our hearts—not because he needs to shore up some weakness in himself or compensate for some deficiency, but because he loves us and seeks the fullness of our joy that can be found only in knowing and praising him, the most magnificent of all Beings. If he is truly for us, he must be for himself!

God is the one Being in all the universe for whom seeking his own praise is the ultimately loving act. For him, self-exaltation is the highest virtue. When he does

all things "for the praise of his glory," he preserves for us
and offers to us the only thing in all the world that can
satisfy our longings. God is for us! And the foundation of
this love is that God has been, is now, and always will be
for himself.

THE GOAL:
BEYOND DESIRE AND DELIGHT

From When I Don't Desire God: How to Fight for Joy, *(Wheaton: Crossway, 2011), 29–31*

Desire and delight have this in common: neither is the Object desired or delighted in. God is. I make this obvious point because all of us from time to time speak loosely and say that the aim of our pursuit is *joy*. Or we say that we want to be happy. Those are not false or evil statements. A Christian means: I aim to pursue joy *in God* so that the infinitely valuable objective reality of the universe, God, will get all the glory possible from my life. "I want to be happy" may be Christian shorthand for "I want to know the One, and the only One, who is in himself all I have ever longed for in all my desires to be happy."

But this loose way of talking can be misleading. Both statements can be taken to mean: The object of our wants is ultimately a psychological experience of happiness without any regard to what makes us happy. In other words, they may mean: The final object of our pursuit is joy itself, rather than the beauty of what we find joy in. This is a very common mistake. Jonathan Edwards warned against it by observing that "there are many affections which do not arise from any light in the understanding. And when it is thus, it is a sure evidence that these affections are not spiritual, let them be ever so high." Our goal is not high affections *per se*. Our goal is to see and savor "the light of the gospel of the glory of Christ, who is the image of God" (2 Cor. 4:4). The affections that arise from that light *are* spiritual. By this Christ-revealing light, we avoid the mistake of simply pursuing joy, not Christ.

C.S. Lewis devoted most of his autobiography, which he called *Surprised by Joy*, to exposing this error by narrating his own mistakes.

> You cannot hope and also think about hoping at
> the same moment; for in hope we look to hope's
> object and we interrupt this by (so to speak)
> turning round to look at the hope itself. ... The
> surest means of disarming an anger or a lust was to
> turn your attention from the girl or the insult and
> start examining the passion itself. The surest way
> of spoiling a pleasure was to start examining your
> satisfaction. ...
>
> I perceived (and this was the wonder of wonders)
> that ... I had been equally wrong in supposing that
> I desired Joy itself. Joy itself, considered simply as
> an event in my own mind, turned out to be of no
> value at all. All the value lay in that of which Joy
> was the desiring. And that object, quite clearly,

was no state of my own mind or body at all. … I asked if Joy itself was what I wanted; and, labeling it "aesthetic experience," had pretended I could answer Yes. But that answer too had broken down. Inexorably Joy proclaimed, "You want—I myself am your want of—something other, outside, not you nor any state of you."[43]

One might ask, in view of this danger, why I would lay so much stress on joy in the Christian life. Why not just talk about God, the object of joy, and leave the experiences to take care of themselves? There are three answers.

One is this: It is not John Piper who commands us to rejoice in the Lord; God does. God elevates this experience of the heart to the level of command, not I. And he does so with blood-earnestness. "Because you did not serve the Lord your God with joyfulness and gladness of heart, … you shall serve your enemies" (Deuteronomy 28:47–48). "God threatens terrible things if we will not be happy."[44] The fight for joy is not a warfare I appointed. God did.

The second answer is that God is most glorified in us when we are most satisfied in him. Therefore, to make pretensions about honoring him more, while not calling people to the most radical, soul-freeing satisfaction in God alone, is self-contradictory. It won't happen. God is glorified in his people by the way we experience him, not merely by the way we think about him. Indeed the devil thinks more true thoughts about God in one day than a saint does in a lifetime, and God is not honored by it. The problem with the devil is not his theology, but his desires. Our chief end is to glorify God, the great Object. We do so most fully when we treasure him, desire him, and delight in him so supremely that we let goods and kindred go and display his love to the poor and the lost.

The third reason we should make much of joy and the pursuit of joy in God is that people do not awaken to how desperate their condition is until they measure their hearts by Christian Hedonism—or whatever you may call it. I have found for thirty years that preaching and teaching about God's demand that we delight in him more than in anything else breaks and humbles people, and makes them desperate for true conversion and true Christianity. Oh, how easy it is to think we are what we ought to be when the emotions are made peripheral! Mere thoughts and mere deeds are manageable by the carnal religious mind. But the emotions—they are the weathercock of the heart. Nothing shows the direction of the deep winds of the soul like the demand for radical, sin-destroying, Christ-exalting joy in God.

But having made my defense, I say again: God and God alone is the final, ultimate goal of our quest. All that God is for us in Jesus is the Object of our quest for joy. When I speak of fighting for joy, I mean joy in God, not joy without reference to God. When I speak of longing for happiness, I mean happiness in all that God is for us in Jesus, not happiness as physical or psychological experience apart from God. Whether we are desiring or delighting, the end of the experience is God.

THE MINISTRY: LOVE SEEKS REWARD

From Desiring God: Meditations of a Christian Hedonist, *Revised edition, (Colorado Springs: Multnomah, 2011), 125*

In Acts 20, Paul gathers for the last time with the elders of the church of Ephesus. There are many tears and much embracing as Paul finishes his farewell address (Acts 20:37). But these tears only accent the poignancy of affection the elders have for one who taught them the joy of ministry.

Paul says, "In all things I have shown you that by working hard in this way we must help the weak and remember the words of the Lord Jesus, how he himself said, 'It is more blessed to give than to receive'" (Acts 20:35). The last thing Paul left ringing in their ears on the beach at Miletus was the ministerial charge of Christian Hedonism: "It is more blessed to give than to receive."

Most people do not feel the hedonistic force of these words because they do not meditate on the meaning of the word *remember.* Literally, Paul says, "In all things I have shown you that, so laboring, it is necessary to help the weak and to remember the words of the Lord Jesus, that he himself said, 'It is more blessed to give than to receive.'"

In other words, Paul says that two things are necessary: (1) to help the weak and (2) to remember that Jesus said it is more blessed to give than to receive. Why are both of these things necessary? Why not just help the weak? Why must one also remember that giving brings blessing?

Most Christians today think that while it is true that giving brings blessing, it is not true that one should "remember" this. Popular Christian wisdom says that blessing will come as a result of giving, but that if you keep this fact before you as a motive, it will ruin the moral value of your giving and turn you into a mercenary. The word remember in Acts 20:35 is a great obstacle to this popular wisdom. Why would Paul tell church elders to keep in mind the benefits of ministry, if in fact their doing so would turn ministers into mercenaries?

Christian Hedonism's answer is that it is necessary to keep in mind the true rewards of ministry so we will not become mercenaries. C.S. Lewis sees this clearly:

> We must not be troubled by unbelievers when
> they say that this promise of reward makes
> the Christian life a mercenary affair. There are
> different kinds of reward. There is the reward
> which has no natural connection with the thing
> you do to earn it, and is quite foreign to the desires
> that ought to accompany those things. Money is
> not the natural reward of love; that is why we call a

man mercenary if he married a woman for the sake of her money. But marriage is the proper reward for a real lover, and he is not mercenary for desiring it. A general who fights well in order to get a peerage is mercenary; a general who fights for victory is not, victory being the proper reward of battle as marriage is the proper reward of love. The proper rewards are not simply tacked on to the activity for which they are given, but are the activity itself in consummation.[45]

I do not see how anyone can honor the word *remember* in Acts 20:35 and still think it is wrong to pursue the reward of joy in the ministry. On the contrary, Paul thinks it is necessary to keep the joy set firmly before us. This is the last and perhaps most important thing he has to say to the Ephesian elders before he departs. "Remember! It is more blessed to give than to receive."

THE CREATION: WIELDING THE WORLD FOR JOY'S SAKE

From "How to Wield the World in the Fight for Joy: Using All Five Senses to See the Glory of God," When I Don't Desire God: How to Fight for Joy, *(Wheaton: Crossway, 2011), 175–208*

In this chapter we wrestle with the relationship between physical causes and spiritual effects. If that sounds vague, consider some examples: Can physical sounds (like music or thunder) cause spiritual effects (like joy in Christ or fear of God)? Can deep ravines produce reverence for Christ? Can a sizzling steak produce satisfaction in Jesus? Everybody knows that music and thunder can cause joy and fear. But can they cause spiritual joy and spiritual fear? Can cliffs and food waken the joy of faith?

Usually the word *spiritual* in the New Testament refers to something or someone that is brought forth by the Holy Spirit, controlled by the Holy Spirit, and directed to the goals of the Holy Spirit, especially the adoration of Christ. But music and thunder and ravines and steak are not the Holy Spirit. They are natural parts of the material creation. What is the relationship between them and spiritual joy?

Or to ask the question another way: In the fight for joy in God can we use physical means? The answer is not easy. That's why I said we would "wrestle" in this chapter. Not all joy exalts Christ. Joy exalts what we rejoice in. If we rejoice in revenge, then we exalt the value of revenge. If we rejoice in pornography, we exalt the value of pornography. Those pleasures are clearly sinful. But what about innocent pleasures? If we rejoice in a beautiful sunrise, what do we exalt? The sunrise? Or the Creator of the sunrise? Or both? And what makes the difference in our hearts and minds?

Many unbelievers are deeply moved to rejoice in the beauty of a sunrise. They do not have the Holy Spirit and do not adore Christ. What is the difference between their joy and spiritual joy? Is the experience the same, and is only our knowledge different? Or is the joy itself different? If so, how?

Is Patience a Fruit of the Spirit or of Sleep?

I take up this question because our everyday experience, as well as the Bible itself, demands it. We know from experience that our spiritual and physical lives are intertwined. Losing sleep increases our impatience and irritability, but the Bible says that *love* is "patient ... it is not irritable" (1 Cor. 13:4–5), and the Bible calls love and patience fruits of the Spirit (Gal. 5:22). So are love and patience fruits of the Spirit, or are they the fruit of sleep?

Even in the Lord's work no one would deny that a rush of adrenaline may accompany some great challenge and give wakefulness and energy for some God-ordained task. But the apostle Paul says, "I toil, struggling with all his energy that *he* powerfully works within me" (Col. 1:29). What is the difference between Paul's physical adrenaline and the powerful energy he feels from Christ? Are they totally separate? Or does Christ somehow work through adrenaline?

The World of Sight and Sound

To grasp the scope of this issue, think of your five senses and the countless sensations they bring and how these affect your emotions and your spiritual life. You have the sense of *sight*, and you see the sky with its clouds and its shades of blue and its horizons of red and orange and its nighttime of moon and stars. You see the earth with its thousands of species of birds and land animals and fish and trees and plants, and its varied terrains of deserts, fields, mountains, plains, forests, hills, canyons, and ravines with rivers. And you see human beings, male and female, short and tall, thin and heavy, with countless hues of skin, no two alike. And you see all that man can make: paintings, sculptures, dramas, movies, machines, buildings, roads, computers, planes, clothing, electrical generators, nuclear plants, artificial hearts, microwave ovens, cell phones, air-conditioning, antibiotics, universities, and governments.

And you have a sense of *hearing*. You hear the sounds of animals: the bird singing, the cat meowing, the dog barking, the snake hissing, the mosquito humming, the frog croaking, the horse neighing and clip-clopping, the pig oinking, the cow mooing, and the rooster crowing. And you hear the sounds of inanimate nature: the ocean waves crashing, the dead tree falling, the landslide plunging, the frozen lake cracking, the volcano exploding, the stream rippling, the thunder rumbling, and the rain pounding. And you hear the sounds of man: talking, laughing, whistling, humming, clapping, crying, groaning, screaming, stomping, singing, playing instruments, pounding nails, revving engines, operating machines, scraping old houses, thumping along with crutches, cooking sizzling hamburgers on a grill, tearing open an envelope, slamming a door, spanking a child, breaking a dish, and mowing the lawn.

The World of Taste and Smell and Touch

And you have a sense of *taste*. You taste hundreds of foods and drinks: sour lemons, sweet honey, sharp cheese, tart grapefruit, salty chips, hot salsa, tangy punch, and countless unique flavors of bananas, milk, nuts, bread, fish, steak, lettuce, chocolate, coffee, green peppers, onions, vanilla ice cream, red Jell-O, and a range of medicines you would rather swallow than taste.

And you have a sense of *smell*. You smell roses, honeysuckle, apple blossoms, lilacs, bread baking, bacon sizzling, toast browning, pizza warming, coffee percolating, clove spice, spilled garbage, raw sewage, paper factories, hog farms, favorite perfumes, newly mown grass, gasoline fumes, pine forests, old books, and cinnamon rolls.

And you have the sense of *touch* and inner sensations. You feel cozy heat curled by a fire, warm flannel sheets on a cold night, a cool breeze on a sunny day, the silk edge of an old blanket, a dog's fur and soft tummy, a foot rub, a shoulder massage, sexual stimulation, the resistance of weightlifting, the pounding of jogging, the dive into a cold mountain lake, the hammer landing on your thumb, the ache in your lower back, the migraine headache, the nausea of seasickness, the kiss of a lover.

Physical Sensations and the Sweetness of God

Any one of these five senses, or any combination of them, can give you emotions. And some of these emotions feel virtually the same as the spiritual emotions we are commanded to have in the Bible: joy (Phil. 4:4), delight (Ps.37:4), gladness (Ps. 67:4), hope (Ps. 42:5), fear (Luke 12:5), grief (Rom. 12:15), desire (1 Pet. 2:2), tenderheartedness (Eph. 4:32), gratitude (Eph. 5:20), etc.

Not only do our senses produce emotions, but the proper or improper use of our bodies can have a huge effect on the way we experience spiritual reality. Rejoicing in the Lord is different when you have nausea than when you are well and singing in a worship service. Proper eating and exercising and sleeping has a marked effect on the mind and its ability to process natural beauty and biblical truth.

So the question must be faced: How do we use the created world around us, including our own bodies, to help us fight for joy in God? In God, I say! Not in nature. Not in music. Not in health. Not in food or drink. Not in natural beauty. How can all these good gifts serve joy in

God, and not usurp the supreme affections of our hearts?

Our situation as physical creatures is precarious. The question we are asking is not peripheral. It addresses the dangerous condition we are in. We are surrounded by innocent things that are ready to become idols. Innocent sensations are one second away from becoming substitutes for the sweetness of God. Should we use mood music and dim lighting and smoke and incense to create an atmosphere that conduces to good feelings and "spiritual" openness? You can feel the dangers of manipulation lurking just below the surface.

But no one escapes the problem. Everybody uses physical means. We all choose some kind of lighting. We all choose some kind of atmosphere, no matter how stark. We all use some kind of music, even if only voice. We all make choices about how we sleep and exercise and eat. And presumably we are not acting like atheists when we make these choices; we believe they have something to do with God. There is no way around the issue. We must all come to terms with how our physical, sensory lives relate to our spiritual joy in God.

Joy Without Brains?

As much as we are sure that our joy in God is more than chemicals and electronic impulses in the brain, we are also sure that, in this present age, we experience this spiritual joy only in connection to a physical body. And the interplay between the two is mysterious. There is, in some strange way, an overlapping of spiritual joy and psychological emotion and physiological event. They are not identical. We know this because God has strong spiritual emotions, like anger (Ps. 80:4) and joy (Zeph. 3:17), but he has no physical body. So there are spiritual emotions that exist independently of physical bodies. Presumably, redeemed people will have strong emotions of adoration and satisfaction at God's right hand after they die and before their bodies are raised from the dead (see Phil. 1:23; Rev. 6:10). So we believe that joy in Christ is not identical with physical brain waves but has an existence above material reality.

In spite of the theoretical popularity of naturalistic evolution, which says all there is in the universe is matter and energy, almost nobody will approve if you put their sense of justice in the same category as a dog's bark. So even those who have no conscious belief in God intuitively operate on the assumption that their emotion of love and their sense of justice are more than electrochemical events in the brain.[46]

Nevertheless, these supra-physical things are linked with our physical brains. And so it is that our joy in God and its physical expression in the brain are inseparable in this mortal life. Spiritual emotions (which are more than physical) can have physical effects, and physical conditions can have spiritual effects.

The Spiritual Orchestra and the Physical Piano

C.S. Lewis thought deeply about the physical and spiritual connection and wrote about it in a sermon called "Transposition." His argument is that the spiritual life of emotion is higher and richer than the material life of physical sensation in the way a symphony orchestra is richer than a piano. When the music of spiritual joy plays in the soul, it gets "transposed" into physical sensations. But since the spiritual "orchestra" is richer and more varied than the physical "piano," the same piano keys have to be used for sounds that in the orchestra are played with different instruments. As physical people with souls, we always experience spiritual emotions at both levels: the orchestra and the piano.

There are at least four reasons why Lewis's analysis is helpful. One is that it explains the fact that introspection can never find spiritual joy in God, but only the residue of physical sensation. The reason is that the moment we turn from focusing on God to focusing on the emotion itself, the emotion is no longer what it was. It leaves its trace only in the physical sensation, not in the spiritual reality. The reality of spiritual joy depends moment by moment on the steadfast seeing of the glory of God.[47]

Second, Lewis's analysis helps explain why the physical sensations we find when we look behind the spiritual emotions of ecstasy and terror seem to be identical. In other words, the physical trembling and the queasy stomach seem to be the same for terror and ecstasy when we analyze them by introspection. Lewis explains that this is what we would expect when an orchestra of emotion is transposed down onto a simpler instrument: very different spiritual emotions must play on the same piano key.

If a good man looks into the face of his fiancée and feels the pleasure of a warm love somewhere—he can't tell if it's in his head or chest, or even more visceral—and then he turns from looking at his lover to find the pleasure—wherever it is—what he will probably find is a physical sensation indistinguishable from lust. The orchestra of love uses the same physical note on the piano that lust uses to play her music, but everyone knows that love and lust are not identical emotions.

But if love and lust are the same at one level—playing on the same piano key of the body—why then do we experience spiritual emotions so differently when they are actually happening—even differently in our bodies? For we do indeed experience lust and love, or terror and ecstasy, as physically different. We experience terror as unpleasant and do not want to repeat it, but we experience ecstasy as pleasant and would like to have it again.

Spiritual Emotion Enters and Transforms Physical Sensation

Lewis answers that in the transposition from the higher to the lower, the spiritual emotion actually enters into the physical sensation so that the sensation becomes part of the higher emotion.

> The very same sensation does not merely
> accompany, nor merely signify, diverse and
> opposite emotions, but becomes part of
> them. The emotion descends bodily, as it were,
> into the sensation and digests, transforms,
> transubstantiates it, so that the same thrill along
> the nerves *is* delight or *is* agony.[48]

This is extremely important. It leads to the third reason why Lewis's analysis is helpful: It answers the materialist-skeptic who looks at the brain waves for "delight" and for "agony" and argues that there can be no reality to the so-called spiritual difference, since both are registered in the brain with the same electrochemical reactions. So he concludes that there is no such thing as spiritual emotions, but only physical sensations. Tragically, that is what millions of modern people claim to believe. But Lewis's analysis shows that this mistake is exactly what we would expect if "transposition" is true. The person who approaches it only "from below" can only hear the piano.

> The brutal man never can by analysis find anything but lust in love … physiology never can find anything in thought except twitchings of the gray matter. … [The materialist] is therefore, as regards the matter in hand, in the position of an animal. You will have noticed that most dogs cannot understand *pointing*. You point to a bit of food on the floor: the dog, instead of looking at the floor, sniffs at your finger. A finger is a finger to him, and that is all. … As long as this deliberate refusal to understand things from above, even where such understanding is possible, continues, it is idle to talk of any final victory over materialism. The critique of every experience from below … will always have the same plausibility. There will always be evidence, and every month fresh evidence, to show that religion is only psychological, justice only self protection, politics only economics, love only lust, and thought itself only cerebral biochemistry.[49]

Fourth, Lewis's analysis helps us understand how to use the world of physical sensation for spiritual purposes. From his contrast between the spiritual orchestra of emotion and the physical piano of sensation we are reminded not to equate spiritual emotion and physical sensation. They are not identical. That is a crucial truth to keep in mind. On the other hand, Lewis also reminds us that spiritual emotions, like joy in God, are only experienced in connection with physical sensations. They are not identical, but they are almost always inseparable. In this earthly life, we are never disembodied souls with only spiritual emotions. We are complex spiritual-physical beings who experience joy in Christ as something more, but almost never less, than physical sensation. I say "almost" to leave open the exceptional possibility that, contrary to his usual way of working, God can do miracles in the midst of suffering, such as ecstasy in the midst of flames, while burning at the stake.

Moreover, Lewis reminds us to be amazed that the higher can actually transform the lower. Spiritual emotions, which are more than physical, can have chemical effects, and not just the reverse. It is true that chemicals can affect emotions. But too seldom do we pray and plan for the spiritual to have chemical effects. As legitimate as sedatives and antidepressants may be in times of clear chemical imbalance, we should not overlook the truth that spiritual reality may also transform the physical and not just vice versa.

Being Intentional in How We Use the Physical for the Sake of Joy in God

But our main question in this chapter is how the lower can affect the higher. That is, how can the physical world of sensation properly assist our joy in Christ? What Lewis has shown us is that God has created us in such a way that there is a correspondence in this life between spiritual emotion and physical experience. God ordained that the brain and the soul intersect and correspond. They are not identical. The physical events in the brain and the spiritual events in the soul do not correspond one to one. But they are interwoven in a way that encourages us to take steps so that the influence flows in both directions for the glory of Christ.

That would mean, for example, that on the one hand we seek by prayer and meditation on God's Word to waken joy in Christ so that it has a healing, strengthening effect on the body. And it would mean, on the other hand, that we use the physical world, including our own bodies, so that, according to the laws of God's creation, joy in Christ will be more intense and more constant. In other words, Lewis has helped us see that there are some legitimate steps we can take at the physical, sensory level in order to properly increase our joy in God.

I say this in spite of the danger mentioned earlier that we run the risk of manipulation (mood music, smoke, and dim lighting) to create "spiritual" emotions, which turn out not to be spiritual at all. There is no running from the responsibility of using physical reality wisely for spiritual ends. Our physical lives will affect our spiritual lives whether we plan it or not. Better to think it through and be intentional.

The Bible Itself Says: See God in the World

Far more important than the wisdom of C.S. Lewis is the biblical wisdom of God. The Bible gives us good evidence that we should indeed be intentional about touching our joy in God with physical means. We have already seen in chapter five that seeing the glory of God is the essential and proper basis of our joy in God. We argued from 2 Corinthians 4:4 that the most central and controlling means of seeing God is by means of hearing the gospel. "The god of this world [Satan] has blinded the minds of the unbelievers, to keep them from seeing *the light of the gospel of the glory of Christ*, who is the image of God." The deepest foundation of our joy, as justified sinners, is that Christ died for our sins and thus revealed the smiling face of God for all who believe. That's the way it is with all the Scriptures: They enable us to see, in them and through them, the glory of God. "The LORD revealed *himself* ... by *the word of the LORD*" (1 Sam. 3:21). God himself stands forth to be spiritually seen and enjoyed "by the word of the LORD."

But the Bible tells us of other means of seeing the glory of God, and therefore other means of wakening and intensifying our joy in him. For example, Psalm 19:1–4:

> The heavens declare the glory of God, and the sky
> above proclaims his handiwork. Day to day pours
> out speech, and night to night reveals knowledge.
> There is no speech, nor are there words, whose

voice is not heard. Their measuring line goes out through all the earth, and their words to the end of the world.

If seeing the glory of God is a proper spiritual cause of our joy in him, then our physical gaze at the heavens—the sun and moon and stars and clouds and sunrises and sunsets and thunderstorms—is a proper means of helping us rejoice in God. So here we have a clear biblical warrant for using the physical world ("the heavens"), by means of the physical organ of sight, to pursue a spiritual effect, namely, seeing the glory of God and experiencing our joy in it.

Other Scriptures make explicit the connection between the physically visible work of God and joy. For example, Psalm 92:4 says, "For you, O Lord, have made me glad by your work; at the works of your hands I sing for joy." I assume that this joy is not idolatrous—that is, I assume it does not terminate on the works themselves, but in and through them, rests on the glory of God himself. The works "declare" the glory of God. They point. But the final ground of our joy is God himself.

Learning from Light in a Toolshed

C.S. Lewis, whose greatest gift was his power to see what few see, described an experience that demonstrated how the physical world helps us see the glory of God.

> I was standing today in the dark toolshed. The
> sun was shining outside and through the crack
> at the top of the door there came a sunbeam.
> From where I stood that beam of light, with the

specks of dust floating in it, was the most striking thing in the place. Everything else was almost pitch-black. I was seeing the beam, not seeing things by it. Then I moved so that the beam fell on my eyes. Instantly the whole previous picture vanished. I saw no toolshed, and (above all) no beam. Instead I saw, framed in the irregular cranny at the top of the door, green leaves moving on the branches of a tree outside and beyond that, 90 odd million miles away, the sun. Looking along the beam, and looking at the beam are very different experiences.[50]

So we can say that when we "look along" the heavens and not just "at" the heavens, they succeed in their aim of "declaring the glory of God." That is, we see the glory *of God*, not just the glory of the heavens. We don't just stand outside and analyze the natural world as a beam, but we let the beam fall on the eyes of our heart, so that we see the source of the beauty—the original Beauty, God himself.

This is the essential key to unlocking the proper use of the physical world of sensation for spiritual purposes. All of God's creation becomes a beam to be "looked along" or a sound to be "heard along" or a fragrance to be "smelled along" or a flavor to be "tasted along" or a touch to be "felt along." All our senses become partners with the eyes of the heart in perceiving the glory of God through the physical world.

So on the one hand, Lewis has shown us that our more-than-physical spiritual emotions are incarnated in our physical sensations, transforming them so that they take on the quality of the emotion. And on the other hand he has shown us that the physical sensations are partners in perceiving the glory of God in the physical world and therefore are means of awakening and shaping those very spiritual emotions. Specifically, joy in God can be awakened by the physical display of God's glory, and that very joy enters and transforms the physical experience of it.

The Apostle Paul Helps Us Use the World in the Fight for Joy

Does the Bible itself give us any explicit help at this point to ensure, as much as possible, that our use of the physical world does in fact help us perceive the glory of God, so that our awakened emotions are not simply natural but spiritual? Yes, the apostle Paul addresses this issue in a fairly direct way in 1 Timothy 4:1–5.

> Now the Spirit expressly says that in later times
> some will depart from the faith by devoting
> themselves to deceitful spirits and teachings of
> demons, [2] through the insincerity of liars whose
> consciences are seared, [3] who forbid marriage and
> require abstinence from foods that God created
> to be received with thanksgiving by those who
> believe and know the truth. [4] For everything
> created by God is good, and nothing is to be
> rejected if it is received with thanksgiving, [5] for *it is
> made holy by the word of God and prayer.*

Notice that Paul predicts the coming of false teachers who have a very negative view of the physical world, particularly sex and food (which together involve all five of our senses). So these false teachers "forbid marriage" and "require abstinence from foods" (v. 3). Paul regards this as rebellion against God, because God's purpose for his good creation, Paul says, is that "nothing is to be rejected" (v. 4).

Instead of rejecting God's creation, Paul says there are two things we should do with it: receive it with thanksgiving (vv. 3–4), and sanctify it (make it holy, v. 5). Consider how each of these connects the physical world with our joy in God.

Gratitude for a Gift Involves Joy in a Giver

The sexual pleasures of the marriage bed and the culinary pleasures of good food, Paul says, are to be "received with thanksgiving." This is directly related to joy in God because of what thanksgiving is. First, gratitude is an emotion, not just a choice. You can make yourself say, "Thank you" when you do not feel gratitude, but everyone knows the difference between the words and the feeling. Gratitude is a spontaneous feeling of gladness because of someone's goodwill toward you. Their gift may not even arrive. It may get lost in the mail. But if you know that you were remembered, and that someone took the trouble to buy you something that you would have enjoyed, and that they sent it to you, you will feel gratitude, even if the gift never comes.

Which means, secondly, that the emotion of gratitude is *directed* toward a giver. Gratitude is occasioned by a gift, but is directed to the giver. Third, gratitude is a kind of joy. It is not a bad feeling or a neutral feeling. It is positive and pleasant. We do not regret feeling gratitude— unless we were deceived, and the gift turns out to be a trap. Begrudging gratitude is an oxymoron. There is no such thing. No one feels gratitude out of duty when they really don't want to. Gratitude is spontaneous and pleasant. It is joy in the goodwill of the giver.

The dominant link in the Bible between our gratitude and God is that God is good. "Oh give thanks to the Lord, for he is good, for his steadfast love endures forever!" (Ps.106:1). The link between our thanks and God's goodness is repeated over and over (Ps. 107:1; 118:1, 29; 136:1; 1 Chron. 16:34; 2 Chron. 7:3; 5:13; Ezra 3:11). What is most significant about this link is that our gratitude is ultimately rooted in what God *is*, not in what he *gives*. The Bible does not say, "Give thanks to the Lord, for he *gives* good things." That is true. The good gifts, like sex and food, are occasions for the gladness of gratitude. But they are not the ultimate focus of our joy. The sensation of pleasure runs up the beam of God's generosity until it stops in the goodness of God himself.

I stress this distinction because it is very easy for us to say we are thankful for the pleasures of sex and food, but never even take God into the picture. When that happens, the joy of sex and food is not joy in God, and is not spiritual, and is not an honor to God for his goodness. Enjoying God's gifts without a consciousness of God is no tribute to God himself. Unbelievers do this all the time. Therefore what Paul is teaching us here is that the proper use of physical pleasures in sex and food is that they send our hearts Godward with the joy of gratitude that finds its firmest ground in the goodness of God himself, not in his gifts.

This means that if, in the providence of God, these gifts are ever taken away—perhaps by the death of a spouse or the demand for a feeding tube—the deepest joy that we had through them will not be taken away, because God is still good (see Hab. 3:17–18).

Sanctifying Sex and Food

After saying that *gratitude* connects the physical world with joy in God, Paul goes on to say that this connection happens when the physical creation is *sanctified*. "Everything created by God is good, and nothing is to be rejected if it is received with thanksgiving, for *it is made holy by the word of God and prayer*" (1 Tim. 4:4–5).

The words "it is made holy" represent one Greek word (*hagiazo*), which sometimes means to set apart for holy use, as when Jesus said, "For which is greater, the gold or the temple that *has made the gold sacred*?" (Matt. 23:17). Here the use of gold in the temple sanctifies it (and is the same word used in 1 Tim. 4:5). The gold is not itself changed, but it is given a God-exalting function by the way it is made part of God's temple. Other times the word *sanctify* means to transform something into a condition that will be suitable for God-exalting purposes, as when Jesus prays for his disciples, asking that God would "Sanctify them in the truth; your word is truth" (John 17:17). So when Paul says that sex and food are sanctified by the Word of God and prayer, it probably means that they are transformed and made suitable for their purpose of wakening and strengthening our God-exalting joy in Christ.

How do the Word of God and prayer bring about

that sanctification of sex and food? The most obvious observation is that the *Word of God* is his speaking to us, and *prayer* is our speaking to him. So the general answer is that sex and food are made useful for God-exalting joy when we listen to what God has to say about them, and then speak back to him our affirmations of his truth and our need for help.

Sanctifying Physical Sensations by the Word of God

But we need to be specific. The relevant truth God speaks to us includes several points:

1. God created sex and food (Gen. 1:27–28; 2:24–25; 3:16).

2. Sex and food are good (Gen. 1:31).

3. Sex and food are intended not only to beget and sustain life, but also to bring us enjoyment. Paul says to Timothy about the wealthy in his congregation, "Charge them not to be haughty, nor to set their hopes on the uncertainty of riches, but on God, who *richly provides us with everything to enjoy*" (1 Tim. 6:17).

4. God's Word tells us that the physical world of nature is declaring the glory of God (Ps. 19:1), so that the enjoyment it brings should rest finally in the beauty of God himself.

5. The Word gives us many particulars about the proper use of sex (e.g., no fornication or adultery) and food (e.g., no addiction or excessive asceticism) and other natural pleasures.

6. The Word of God tells us that we are sinners and do not deserve anything but the wrath of God (Rom. 1:18; 3:9), and therefore the joy of seeing the glory of God in and through the pleasures of sex and food is an absolutely free gift bought with the blood of Jesus Christ (Rom. 8:32).

Knowing and affirming these truths from God's Word transforms sex and food from mere physical pleasures into partners in *revelation* and *rejoicing*. These physical sensations partner with the spiritual eyes of our hearts to perceive the *revelation* of God's glory in creation and to promote our *rejoicing* in him. When Paul said in Titus 1:15, "To the pure all things are pure," he had something like this in mind. He contrasts the pure with "the defiled and *unbelieving*." That links Titus 1:15 with 1 Timothy 4:3 where Paul says that sex and food are "to be received with thanksgiving by *those who believe* and know the truth." In other words, sex and food are designed for *believers*, the pure in heart. For "to the pure all things are pure."

To those who submit gladly to the truth of God about themselves as sinners, and about Christ as the Savior, and about the Holy Spirit as the Sanctifier, and about God the Father as Creator, to them sex and food are sanctified. That is, they are pure. They are not unclean idols competing for our affections, which belong supremely to God. They are instead pure partners in the revelation of God's glory. They are beams of his goodness *along* which the pure in heart see God (Matthew 5:8).

Sanctifying Physical Sensations by Prayer

Thus sex and food and other natural physical delights are

sanctified "by the word of God" (1 Tim. 4:5). But the same verse also says they are sanctified by "prayer." One way that prayer sanctifies sex and food and other physical sensations is by expressing to God our thanks for his goodness. But prayer has another role. Prayer also means asking God for the illumination of the eyes of our heart so that, in and through our physical sensations, we would see the glory of God. Prayer acknowledges that we cannot achieve our own purity. We cannot sanctify our own sensations. We cannot open our own eyes. And therefore we cannot enjoy God in all his gifts without the enabling grace that God gives in answer to prayer. Therefore we pray that the truth will have its sanctifying effect by the power of God's Spirit.

Thus prayer and the Word of God together sanctify sex and food— and every other good gift in this world. The physical reality of food and human bodies, along with their physical sensations, become pure partners in the revelation of God's glory and the wakening of our joy in him.

The Direct Use of the World in the Fight for Joy

When we consider carefully how to use the physical world for the advancement of our joy in God, we realize that there is a *direct* use to be made of nature and an *indirect* use. The *direct* use is when we take steps to see and hear and smell and taste and touch God's creation (and man's representation of it in art) in order to perceive the glory of God more fully. The *indirect* use is when we take steps to keep our bodies and minds as fit as we can for spiritual use. Let's consider these in turn.

The *direct* use of the physical world in our fight for joy

may be a trip to the Grand Canyon, or rising early enough to see a sunrise, or attending a symphony, or reading a historical novel, or studying physics, or memorizing a poem, or swimming in the ocean, or eating a fresh pineapple, or smelling a gardenia blossom, or putting your hand through your wife's hair, or watching Olympic gymnastics finals. All these and a thousand things like them are *direct* ways of using the natural world to perceive more of the glory of God.

The Glory of God Is an Overwhelmingly Happy Thing

Even though some encounters with God are terrible, it seems plain from Scripture that God wants us to rejoice in the glory we see in nature. I base this, for example, on Psalm 19. After saying, "The heavens declare the glory of God," David reaches for language to show the joy being communicated by the heavens. He says that the sun "comes out like a bridegroom leaving his chamber, and, like a strong man, runs its course with joy. Its rising is from the end of the heavens, and its circuit to the end of them, and there is nothing hidden from its heat" (Ps. 19:5–6).

Clearly this poet wants us to see and to feel that when the sun pours forth speech about the glory of God, the message is that the glory of God is an overwhelmingly happy thing. Why else would he say it is like a bridegroom coming out of his chamber? The point here is not merely that the bridegroom is decked out in the finest clothes and surrounded by his noble groomsmen. The point is that this is the happiest day of his life. This is the fulfillment of dreams. This is the beginning of a whole new kind of joy. That's what the glory of God is like. That's the message we should hear when we see the sun rise with lavish red and gold and lavender in the eastern sky. God's glory is a happy thing—like the happiness of a bridegroom on his wedding day.

This is even more explicit in the other picture David uses at the end of verse 5. When the sun rises and pours forth speech about the glory of God, it is like a strong man that runs his race *with joy*. How can we not think of Eric Liddell in that great scene from the film *Chariots of Fire* as he takes that last turn in the race for the glory of God, and his arms drive like living pistons, and his head goes back in that utterly unorthodox position, and every fiber in his body does just what it was made to do, and the smile breaks out across his face, and everything in Eric Liddell cries, "Glory to God!"

That's what the glory of God is like—it's like the happiest day of your life; it's like every muscle and every tendon and every ligament and every organ and all your mind and your emotions working just the way they were created to work on the day of triumph. The glory of God is the happiest reality in the universe.

Don't Neglect the Gift of Human Representations of God's Glory

In our fight for joy, we must not neglect the ministry of God to our souls in the world that he has made. We should make direct use of the world to see and savor the glory of God wherever he has displayed it. This includes the efforts of man, by his design and art, to represent something of

God's glory. Even those who do not believe in God often sense that there is more to see in what they see. The Bible insists that every human being, even when suppressing the knowledge of God, does indeed "know God" and has "clearly perceived" his attributes in the things he has made.

> For what can be known about God is plain to them, because God has shown it to them. For his invisible attributes, namely, his eternal power and divine nature, have been clearly perceived, ever since the creation of the world, in the things that have been made. So they are without excuse. For although they knew God, they did not honor him as God. (Rom.1:19–21)

This means that even the artistic works of unbelievers sometimes penetrate through the commonplace to the outskirts of the glory of God. Believers whose hearts are purified by the grace of Christ may see from this vantage point vastly more than the unbeliever. So even the unbelieving artist may unwittingly assist us in seeing and savoring the glory of God in the world he has made.

The Power of Human Words to Make the World a Cause of Joy

It is not a mistake that so much of the Bible is written in poetry. Nor is it a mistake that there are so many biblical metaphors and similes. The lesson is that God has ordained for poetry to pierce and portray what colorless language cannot do. The human heart moves irrepressibly toward poetry because it knows intuitively that the natural world is not all there is. The heart may not even believe that the heavens are telling the glory of God. But the heart knows, deep down, that the heavens are telling something more than meets the physical eye.

Therefore, in our fight for joy it may often be helpful to read penetrating literature and see powerful drama. Not because they can ever rival or replace the Scriptures, but because they are part of the God-revealing creation and its reflection. God did not put us in the world to ignore it, but to use it wisely. From the beginning, human beings have discovered that the reflection of the world in human art wakens us to the world itself and what the world is saying about God. Echoes can waken us to the shout of reality, and poetry can give us eyes to see. If we weren't afflicted with persistent sleepiness of soul, we might see all the glory there is in nature. But as it is, we need help from creative artists.

Richard Foster is justified in writing:

> I am concerned that our reading and our writing
> is gravitating to the lowest common denominator
> so completely that the great themes of majesty and
> nobility and felicity are made to seem trite, puny,
> pedestrian. ... I am concerned about the state of the
> soul in the midst of all the cheap sensory overload
> going on today. You see, without what Alfred North
> Whitehead called "an habitual vision of greatness,"
> our soul will shrivel up and lose the capacity for
> beauty and mystery and transcendence. ...
>
> But it isn't just the substance of what we say (or
> write or read or hear or see) that concerns me. It

is the way we say it. To write pedantically about radiance or infinity or ubiquity stunts the mind and cramps the soul. To find the right word, to capture the perfect image, awakens the spirit and enlarges the soul. Mark Twain noted that the difference between the right word and the almost right word is like the difference between the lightning and a lightning bug.[51] ... The ancient Hebrew prophets cared enough about their message that they frequently delivered it in poetic form. May new prophets arise in our day that will call us to faithful living in words that are crisp and clear and imaginative.[52]

And when they arise, one way that we fight for joy in God is to read what they write. The heavens are telling the glory of God. Seeing it is the ground of our joy. And often reading what others have seen wakens us to see what they saw, or even more.

Fighting for Joy with Sights and Sounds That Humans Make

Of course, words are not the only way that artists waken others to the glory of what they have seen. There is visual art (drawing, painting, sculpture, photography, film), and there is music. I will not say much here because I am out of my element. What I know about art and music I know from experience, not formal study. I am a witness, not a judge. And what I testify to is the power of visual art, and especially music. As it is with creative writing, so it is with visual art and music: they have the potential to awaken the mind and heart to aspects of God's glory that were not perceived before. Paintings or photographs of mountains and streams can call forth a sense of wonder and peace. If we are willing to "look along" (not just "at") these pictures, as Lewis taught us, our eyes will run up the beams to the original Glory, and the wonder and peace will rest finally in the wonderful and peaceful mountains and streams of God's power and mercy.

Music, it seems to me, is the most complex art of all. Who can really explain what happens when music works its power? Its transforming effects are documented in cases ranging from Parkinson's disease[53] to plants.[54] As with all things in nature and in the hands of fallen man, it can be used to reveal or conceal the glory of God—to corrupt the mind or illumine the mind. At its best, music echoes a true perception of some facet of God's glory. The ambiguity of the medium itself, combined with cultural and social and personal associations, complicates the display of that glory in sound.

I recall reading the story of a tribal person, with no previous exposure to Western culture, who was flown to Europe and taken to a performance of Handel's *Messiah*. He sat almost the whole time covering his ears with his hands because, as he explained later, it was just so much noise to his ears. That is an extreme illustration of the complexity of communicating with music. Nevertheless, the power is there, and it works every day for good and for ill. My point is that in the fight for joy it is good and right to pursue a deeper sense of God's glory with the help of music.

Wielding the Weapon of Music in the Fight for Joy in God

If this were not right, the Bible would not command us so often to sing (e.g., Ex.15:21; 1 Chron. 16:23; Ps. 96:1) or to play on instruments (e.g., Ps. 33:2–3; 57:8; 81:2; 150). Music seems to be woven into worship and the world of nature. Among the many creatures that God has made in his wisdom (Ps. 104:24) are the birds that God has taught to sing: "Beside [the springs] the birds of the heavens dwell; they sing among the branches" (Ps. 104:12). Surely God has not created music as a pointless distraction from rational apprehensions of God. Surely, this too is part of the creation that is "declaring the glory of God."

To wield music well in the fight for joy we should be filled with the Word of God, so that our minds are shaped by biblical truth. If our mind and heart have been molded by the contours of God's character and humbled by the grace of the gospel, we will discern better what sounds reveal and correspond to the varied glories of God. And since this discernment depends so much on cultural contexts and personal backgrounds, we will need not only a grasp of musical richness, but also deep theological grounding in God-centered truth, sensitivity to different cultures, awareness of the dynamics of the heart, and profound love for people of all kinds.

We must make it our aim that the joy awakened by music be joy in God. Not all pleasures of music are pleasures in God. The effort to delight in God through music will involve a prior shaping of the mind by the Word, so that structures of sound that do not conform to

God's character are not pleasing in the first place. Then the effort to delight in God through music will also involve a thoughtful testing *after* the music has already awakened joy. Is this joy, we ask, rooted in something good about God? Is it shaping my emotions into a Christ-exalting configuration? Is it stirring my desires to know Christ better and love him more and show him to others at the cost of my own comfort? So *before* and *after* music has its immediate effect, we pursue the goal that music makes us more glad in the glory of God.[55]

Fighting for Joy with the Wonder of the Commonplace

I don't want to give the impression that in our fight for joy one must always make special plans to pursue such revelations of God's glory— like a trip to the mountains or a theater. Most of the time we should simply open our eyes (and ears and noses and skin and taste buds). Not that this takes no effort. Clearly human beings have a strange malady that makes the ordinary glories of each day almost invisible, and certainly less interesting than their imitations in theaters and television. There are more oohs and aahs over the visual effects on a thirty-foot theater screen than over the night sky and the setting sun. Why is it so hard for us to feel wonder at the everyday glory when clearly it is more spectacular than the man-made imitation?

Clyde Kilby, a former literature teacher at Wheaton College, who had a great influence on me when I was there, gave this answer:

The fall of man can hardly be more forcefully felt than simply in noting what we all do with a fresh snowfall or the first buds of spring. On Monday they fill us with delight and meaning and on Tuesday we ignore them. No amount of shouting to us that this is all wrong changes the fact for very long. ... Only some aesthetic power which is akin to God's own creativity has the capability for renewal, for giving us the power to see.[56]

This is a tragic condition captured by the proverb that "familiarity breeds contempt"—or that familiarity breeds blindness to ordinary and obvious beauty. But surely redemption through Jesus Christ means that we will be freed from that proverb someday. And since our redemption has already begun in this age, by the power of the Holy Spirit, Christians ought to have better eyes than people in general for seeing the wonders that day and night pour forth. We ought to be the kind of people who walk out of the house in the morning with the same sense of expectancy that we take into the theater—only more.

Chesterton's Elephantine Pursuit of the Obvious

Once when we were discussing in class this issue of human blindness to everyday wonders, Dr. Kilby recommended that we all read G.K. Chesterton's book *Orthodoxy*. He said it would do more to help us see the glory of God in everyday life than anything he could say. I got it and read it. I recommend it, not because its theology is always right (he is Roman Catholic and does not like Calvinism), but because it holds out hope of seeing the divine glory in the obvious better than any book I know.

Chesterton says of the book that "it recounts my elephantine adventures in pursuit of the obvious."[57] He identifies one of the great causes of our blindness as self-absorption. He says that a person who is becoming morbid over fears and preoccupations about what others think of him needs the liberation from his illusion that anyone gives a hoot!

> How much happier you would be if you only knew that these people cared nothing about you! How much larger your life would be if your self could become smaller in it; if you could really look at other men with common curiosity and pleasure; if you could see them walking as they are in their sunny selfishness and their virile indifference! You would begin to be interested in them because they were not interested in you. You would break out of this tiny and tawdry theater in which your own little plot is always being played, and you would find yourself under a freer sky, in a street full of splendid strangers.[58]

In other words, what we need is a kind of childlikeness. And romantic tales are often used to awaken it.

> When we are very young children we don't need fairy tales: we only need tales. Mere life is interesting enough. A child of seven is excited by being told that Tommy opened a door and saw a dragon. But a child of three is excited by being told that Tommy opened a door. Boys like romantic

tales; but babies like realistic tales—because
they find them romantic. ... This proves that even
nursery tales only echo an almost pre-natal leap of
interest and amazement. These tales say that apples
are golden only to refresh the forgotten moment
when we found that they were green. They make
rivers run with wine only to make us remember, for
one wild moment, that they run with water.[59]

The point is that Christ frees us from self-preoccupation
and gives us—yes, only very gradually—a childlikeness
that can see the sheer wonder of the staggering strangeness
of the ordinary. Chesterton said that this discovery for
him was captured in a riddle: "What did the first frog
say?" Answer: "Lord, how you made me jump!"[60] In
another place he says that he came to the point where what
amazed him was not the strangeness of people's noses,
but that they had noses in the first place. In becoming
more childlike and more able to see glory in the wonder
of the ordinary and the routine, he points out that we are
becoming more like God.

[Children] always say, "Do it again," and the
grown-up person does it again until he is nearly
dead. For grown-up people are not strong enough
to exult in monotony. But perhaps God is strong
enough to exult in monotony. It is possible that
God says every morning, "Do it again" to the sun;
and every evening, "Do it again" to the moon. It
may not be automatic necessity that makes all
daisies alike; it may be that God makes every
daisy separately, but has never got tired of making

them. It may be that he has the eternal appetite of infancy; for we have sinned and grown old, and our Father is younger than we.[61]

I linger over this point—that seeing the glory of God may not require making a trip to the mountains or buying a ticket to the theater, but only opening our eyes—because I believe untold resources for mental health and spiritual joy in God lie all around us if we would but open our eyes.

Kilby's Prescription for Using the World in the Fight for Joy

At the end of his life, my teacher Clyde Kilby came to Minneapolis and gave a lecture on how he intended to use the world in the fight for joy. It was the last time I heard him, and the message that he bequeathed to us who listened was the same legacy he had left to me when I was in his college classes. He summed up his talk with eleven resolutions. I commend them to you as one way of overcoming our bent toward blindness for the wonders of the ordinary.

1. At least once every day I shall look steadily up at the sky and remember that I, a consciousness with a conscience, am on a planet traveling in space with wonderfully mysterious things above me and about me.

2. Instead of the accustomed idea of a mindless and endless evolutionary change to which we can neither add nor subtract, I shall suppose the universe guided by an Intelligence which, as Aristotle said of Greek drama, requires a beginning, a middle and an end. I think

this will save me from the cynicism expressed by Bertrand Russell before his death, when he said: "There is darkness without and when I die there will be darkness within. There is no splendor, no vastness anywhere, only triviality for a moment, and then nothing."[62]

3. I shall not fall into the falsehood that this day, or any day, is merely another ambiguous and plodding twenty-four hours, but rather a unique event filled, if I so wish, with worthy potentialities. I shall not be fool enough to suppose that trouble and pain are wholly evil parentheses in my existence but just as likely ladders to be climbed toward moral and spiritual manhood.

4. I shall not turn my life into a thin straight line which prefers abstractions to reality. I shall know what I am doing when I abstract,[63] which of course I shall often have to do.

5. I shall not demean my own uniqueness by envy of others. I shall stop boring into myself to discover what psychological or social categories I might belong to. Mostly I shall simply forget about myself and do my work.

6. I shall open my eyes and ears. Once every day I shall simply stare at a tree, a flower, a cloud, or a person. I shall not then be concerned at all to ask *what* they are but simply be glad that they are. I shall joyfully allow them the mystery of what [C.S.] Lewis calls their "divine, magical, terrifying and ecstatic" existence.

7. I shall sometimes look back at the freshness of vision I

had in childhood and try, at least for a little while, to be, in the words of Lewis Carroll, the "child of the pure unclouded brow, and dreaming eyes of wonder."[64]

8. I shall follow Darwin's[65] advice and turn frequently to imaginative things such as good literature and good music, preferably, as Lewis suggests, an old book and timeless music.

9. I shall not allow the devilish onrush of this century to usurp all my energies but will instead, as Charles Williams suggested, "fulfill the moment as the moment." I shall try to live well just now because the only time that exists is just now.

10. If for nothing more than the sake of a change of view, I shall assume my ancestry to be from the heavens rather than from the caves.

11. Even if I turn out to be wrong, I shall bet my life in the assumption that this world is not idiotic, neither run by an absentee landlord, but that today, this very day, some stroke is being added to the cosmic canvas that in due course I shall understand with joy as a stroke made by the architect who calls himself Alpha and Omega.

Fighting for Joy by the Indirect Use of the World

I mentioned earlier that in our fight for joy there is a *direct* use to be made of nature and an *indirect* use. We've been talking mainly about the *direct* use—that is, when we take steps to see and hear and smell and taste and touch God's creation (and man's representation of it in art) in order to perceive the glory of God more fully. But with Kilby's eleven resolutions we have begun to cross over to the *indirect* use of nature. What I mean by the *indirect* use of nature is the steps we take to make our bodies and minds as proficient as possible in their role as physical partners in perceiving the glory of God.

Keep in mind that when the Bible says that "the heavens *declare* the glory of God" (Psalm 19:1), it is clear that the heavens are *not* the glory of God. They "declare" it or display it. They are the beam *along* which we look till our eyes run up to the spiritual beauty of God himself. Thus we see the heavens with our bodily eyes, and we experience the sensations of that sight in our physical brains. Yet we perceive the glory of God with our spiritual eyes.

Jonathan Edwards describes this kind of joy (through creation) in God as he ponders what heaven will be like. Will we enjoy only God there, or will we enjoy other things as well? What does the psalmist mean when he declares, "I say to the LORD, 'You are my LORD; *I have no good apart from you*'" (Ps. 16:2), or "Whom have I in heaven but you? And *there is nothing on earth that I desire besides you*" (Ps. 73:25)? Edwards answers:

> The redeemed will indeed enjoy other things; they
> will enjoy the angels, and will enjoy one another:
> but that which they shall enjoy in the angels, or
> each other, or in anything else whatsoever, that
> will yield them delight and happiness, will be what
> will be seen of God in them.[66]

This is what we pray toward even now—that all our joy in the things of this world would be because, in and through them, we see more of the glory of God. Spiritual beauty is perceived in and through physical beauty but is not identical with it. This is why I call the body with its sensations the physical *partner* in perceiving the glory of God in the natural world.

Edwards gives us an illustration of the indirect use of nature in the fight for joy. He writes:

> When the body enjoys the perfections of health and strength, the motion of the animal spirits [physical responses] are not only brisk and free but also harmonious. There is a regular proportion in the motion from all parts of the body that begets delight in the inner soul and makes the body feel pleasantly all over. God has so excellently contrived the nerves and parts of the human body. But few men since the fall, especially since the flood, have health to so great a perfection as to have much of this harmonious motion. When it is enjoyed, one whose nature is not very much vitiated and depraved is very much assisted thereby in every exercise of body or mind. *And it fits one for the contemplation of more exalted and spiritual excellencies and harmonies, as music does.*[67]

What this means is that there are conditions of the body and the mind that are more conducive than others to the perception of spiritual beauty. This is the main reason for trying to handle our bodies with a wise measure of discipline. We want to see and savor the divine glory that God declares in the heavens and on the earth and in food and sexual intimacy and music and poetry and art. And

Edwards is saying that there is a condition of the body that hinders or helps the perception of God's excellencies.

The Grace of Glory Revealed to Suffering Christians

Immediately I feel a qualification rising in my own mind. Beaten and battered prisoners for Christ often have extraordinary views of the beauty and sustaining sweetness of Christ. They are without food or warmth or cleanliness or any physical comfort. Yet they call persecution sweet names and put to shame most of us who are fit and hardy. They often have a superior spiritual sight in their broken health and simple meals.

So please don't interpret this final part of the chapter as a kind of chipper health and happiness regimen. The question is not whether God can reveal himself in precious ways to those who suffer. He can and does. It is possible, as the Bible says, to rejoice in tribulation (Rom. 5:3). "If you are insulted for the name of Christ, you are blessed, because the Spirit of glory and of God rests upon you" (1 Pet. 4:14). The question is what we should do during times when we can choose our own lifestyle of eating and exercising and resting. In what indirect ways can we improve the ability of our bodies and minds for their partnership in perceiving the glory of God?

Eating Right for the Sake of Joy in God

We have already touched on fasting in the previous chapter. There is a paradox here. By saying no to a physical appetite we say yes to the body's ability to help us see the glory of God. A full stomach may say thanks for the food;

but an empty stomach may see heavenly food more clearly. That's what Paul seems to imply about the sexual appetite when he says to Christian husbands and wives, "Do not deprive one another, except perhaps by agreement for a limited time, that you may devote yourselves to prayer" (1 Cor. 7:5). It really doesn't take much time to have sexual intercourse; so the issue is not to *save time* for prayer. The issue seems to be that fasting from legitimate sexual pleasure tunes the body in a unique way for communion with God. I say this even while remembering how earnestly we contended earlier in this chapter for seeing the glory of God in the very act of sexual intimacy and in the very act of eating. Both are true.

Sereno Dwight tells us that Jonathan Edwards "carefully observed the effects of the different sorts of food, and selected those which best suited his constitution, and rendered him most fit for mental labor."[68] Thus he abstained from every quantity and kind of food that made him sick or sleepy. Edwards had set this pattern when he was twenty-one years old when he wrote in his diary, "By a sparingness in diet, and eating as much as may be what is light and easy of digestion, I shall doubtless be able to think more clearly, and shall gain time."[69] Hence he was "Resolved, to maintain the strictest temperance in eating and drinking."[70]

The point here is not to commend the particulars of Edwards's eating habits. The point is that we can be intentional about how our eating affects the ability of our body to be a helpful partner in seeing the glory of God. We live in an era of eating disorders.[71] I am not eager to create another one. I commend balance. Put the following two texts beside each other. On the one hand, Paul made food and drink clearly secondary: "The kingdom of God is not a matter of eating and drinking but of righteousness and peace and joy in the Holy Spirit" (Rom. 14:17). But on the other hand, he said, in regard to food, "I will not be enslaved by anything" (1 Cor. 6:12). In the balance of those two truths we can find a way to eat that will provide both the denial and the delight that will fit us for seeing the glory of God in the Word and in the world.

Exercise As an Indirect Fight for Joy

The Bible has little to say about physical exercise, not because it's not important for modern sedentary people, but mainly because, in the biblical world of walking and farming and manual labor, the lack of physical exercise was not a problem. The call today is for spiritual wisdom based on biblical principles and contemporary medical knowledge.

The biblical principles would include the following:

1. Our bodies belong to Christ and are meant to glorify him (1 Cor. 6:19–20).

2. Laziness is wrong and self-destructive (Prov. 21:25).

3. Christians should be free from any enslaving habits (1 Cor. 6:12).

4. Hard work is a virtue and brings rewards (2 Tim. 2:6).

5. Advance usually comes through affliction (Acts 14:22).

6. All Christ-exalting efforts to be healthy flow from faith in the gospel of Jesus Christ (Gal. 6:14).

"No pain, no gain" is an idea that could be documented from all over the Bible, especially the sacrifice of Christ.

Contemporary medical knowledge would include the fact that obesity kills and contributes to dozens of ailments. Not all obesity is self-inflicted. Some medical conditions make it virtually impossible to avoid. But most of obesity is self-inflicted, and this kind of self-destruction does not enhance the ability of the body or the mind to see and savor the glory of God in this world, or the glory of Christ who endured the cross by postponing the feast till the age to come (Heb. 12:2).

Another aspect of medical knowledge that should shape our wisdom about exercising is that consistent exercise has refining effects on our mental and emotional stability. One medical report sums up the benefits like this:

> The psychological and emotional benefits from exercise are numerous, and many experts now believe that exercise is a viable and important component in the treatment of emotion disorders. A 1999 review of multiple studies found, across the board, that exercise advances the treatment of clinical depression and anxiety. ... Yet another study found that regular brisk walking cut the incidence of sleep disturbances in half in people who suffer from them. ... Either brief periods of intense training or prolonged aerobic workouts raise levels of chemicals in the brain, such as endorphins, adrenaline, serotonin, and dopamine, that produce feelings of pleasure. ... Aerobic

exercise is also linked with improved mental vigor, including reaction time, acuity, and math skills. Exercising may even enhance creativity and imagination. According to one study, older people who are physically fit respond to mental challenges just as quickly as unfit young adults.[72]

Again keep in mind that the aim of this chapter and this book is not maximal physical health. Nor is it to help you find ways to get the best buzz for your brain. None of that is of any interest to me. My aim is that you will find a way of life that enables you to use your mind and your five senses as effective partners in seeing the glory of God, and that you be so satisfied in him that you are willing to risk your health and your life to make him known. It may seem paradoxical, but that's the way it is: the right use of your body and your mind may enable you to see so much of God that you would sacrifice your life for Christ.

Rest As a Weapon in the Fight for Joy

Finally, if we would see the glory of God, we must rest. For all his talk about spending and being spent, Charles Spurgeon, the nineteenth-century London pastor, counsels us to fight for joy by resting and taking a day off and opening ourselves to the healing powers that God has put in the world of nature.

For us pastors, he says, "Our Sabbath is our day of toil, and if we do not rest upon some other day we shall break down."[73] Spurgeon himself kept, when possible, Wednesday as his day of rest.[74] More than that, Spurgeon said to his students,

It is wisdom to take occasional furlough. In the long run, we shall do more by sometimes doing less. On, on, on for ever, without recreation may suit spirits emancipated from this "heavy clay", but while we are in this tabernacle, we must every now and then cry halt, and serve the Lord by holy inaction and consecrated leisure. Let no tender conscience doubt the lawfulness of going out of harness for a while.[75]

And when we take time away from the press of duty, Spurgeon recommends that we breathe country air and let the beauty of nature do its appointed work. He confesses that "sedentary habits have a tendency to create despondency ... especially in the months of fog." And then he counsels:

> He who forgets the humming of the bees among the heather, the cooing of the wood-pigeons in the forest, the song of birds in the woods, the rippling of rills among the rushes, and the sighing of the wind among the pines, needs not wonder if his heart forgets to sing and his soul grows heavy. A day's breathing of fresh air upon the hills, or a few hours' ramble in the beech woods' umbrageous calm, would sweep the cobwebs out of the brain of scores of our toiling ministers who are now but half alive. A mouthful of sea air, or a stiff walk in the wind's face, would not give grace to the soul, but it would yield oxygen to the body, which is the next best. ... The ferns and the rabbits, the streams and the trouts, the fir trees and the squirrels, the

primroses and the violets, the farm-yard, the new-mown hay, and the fragrant hops—these are the best medicine for hypochondriacs, the surest tonics for the declining, the best refreshments for the weary. For lack of opportunity, or inclination, these great remedies are neglected, and the student becomes a self-immolated victim.[76]

Getting Older in the Fight for Joy

We must keep an eye on the apostolic command, "Keep a close watch on yourself" (1 Tim. 4:16). One reason we must watch ourselves closely is that we change over the years. What was wise eating and exercising and resting in the early years is no longer wise. As I write, I am finishing my twenty-fourth year at the church I serve. I am moving toward my fifty-ninth birthday. I have watched my body and my soul with some care over these years and have noticed some changes. They are partly owing to changing circumstances, but much is owing to a changing body.

I cannot eat as much as I used to without gaining unhelpful weight. My body does not metabolize the same way it used to. Another change is that I am emotionally less resilient when I lose sleep. There were early days when I could work without regard to sleep and feel energized and motivated. In more recent years my threshold for despondency is lower on less sleep. For me, adequate sleep is not just a matter of staying healthy. It's a matter of staying in the ministry—I'm tempted to say it's a matter of persevering as a Christian. I know it is irrational that my future should look so bleak when I get only four or five hours of sleep several nights in a row. But rational or irrational, that is a fact. And I must live within the limits of facts. Therefore we must watch the changes in our bodies. In the fight for joy we must be wise in the adjustments we make.

Spurgeon was right when he said:

> The condition of your body must be attended to. ... [A] little more ... common sense would be a great gain to some who are ultra spiritual, and attribute all their moods of feeling to some supernatural cause when the real reason lies far nearer to hand. Has it not often happened that dyspepsia [indigestion] has been mistaken for backsliding, and bad digestion has been set down as a hard heart?[77]

I once struggled with the truth that joy is a fruit of the Holy Spirit (Gal. 5:22), because I knew from experience that it is also a "fruit" of a good night's rest. In other words, I was more gloomy on little rest and more happy on good rest. What brought light to this perplexity is that one of the ways the Spirit produces his fruit in our lives is by humbling us enough to believe we are not God and that God can run the world without our staying up too late and getting up too early. God has united the body and the spirit in such a way that careless uses of the body will ordinarily diminish our sight of the hope-giving glory of God. Not surprisingly, therefore, our joy in God usually decreases with inadequate rest.

All the World a Witness to the Glory of God

Joy in God is not the same as joy in sex or a sizzling steak or deep ravines or powerful music. But God's will is that all these joys—and every part of his good creation—declare the glory of God. All the world, and even the imperfect representations of it in human art, is a witness to the glory of God. That glory is the ultimate ground of all human gladness. Therefore, the created world is a holy weapon in the fight for joy. But it must be "made holy by the word of God and prayer" (1 Tim. 4:5). To help you do that has been my aim in this chapter.

THE INCOMPARABLE: GOD IS HAPPY AND FREE

From The Pleasures of God: Meditations on God's Delight in Being God, *(Colorado Springs: Multnomah, 2012), 39–40*

I love the image that C.S. Lewis gives of God's sovereign freedom in creation. It shows how the good pleasure of his heart to create and save is the happy overflow of his all-sufficiency. Lewis says,

> To be sovereign of the universe is no great matter to God. ... We must keep always before our eyes that vision of Lady Julian's in which God carried in His hand a little object like a nut, and that nut was "all that is made." God, who needs nothing, loves into existence wholly superfluous creatures in order that He may love and perfect them.[78]

This connection between power and pleasure is behind 1 Timothy 6:15–16, where the apostle Paul calls God, "the blessed and only Sovereign, the King of kings and Lord of lords, who alone has immortality." We saw in chapter 1 that "blessed" (makarios) means "happy" (1 Tim. 1:11). Thus Paul is speaking of the "happy and only Sovereign." Notice what is stressed in calling God "blessed" or "happy." God's sole and unique power over all other powers is stressed. First, he is called the "only Sovereign"—not just the Sovereign, but the only Sovereign. In other words, he has no serious competitors for his power. He is the only "powerful one."

Then Paul says that this happy God is "King of kings." Again the point is that he is over all other royal authorities that might seem to challenge his power and his freedom to act as he pleases. Then Paul says that he is "Lord of lords." If there are any gods or lords (and there are!), Paul emphasizes that there are none that can successfully overthrow the power and freedom of the Lord of lords (1 Cor. 8:5–6). Finally Paul says that "he alone has immortality." God is in a class by himself. All other beings depend upon his creative power for existence and life (Acts 17:25). He depends upon no one.

All of this teaches that the happiness of God is rooted in his utterly unique power and authority in the universe. He is the "only Sovereign," and therefore he is the happy Sovereign, because there is none that can frustrate what he aims to do according to his good pleasure. C.S. Lewis puts it like this: "The freedom of God consists in the fact that no cause other than himself produces his acts and no external obstacle impedes them—that his own goodness is the root from which they all grow and his own omnipotence the air in which they all flower."[79]

NOTES

1   Alister McGrath, *The Intellectual World of C.S. Lewis* (Oxford: Wiley-Blackwell, 2013), 2.

2   Ibid., 5.

3   Walter Hooper, ed., *C.S. Lewis Poems* (New York: Harcourt, Brace & World, 1964), vi.

4   The entire list is given later in this book.

5   Hooper, *Poems*, vii.

6   C.S. Lewis, "Christianity and Literature," in *Christian Reflections*, ed. Walter Hooper (Grand Rapids: William B. Eerdmans Publishing Company, 1967), 10.

7   Ibid.

8   Ibid., 14.

9   Ibid., 15.

10   Ibid., 24.

11   Spoken by William Empson, quoted in Alister McGrath, *C.S. Lewis: A Life* (Carold Stream, Illinois: Tyndale House Publishers, Inc., 2013), 166.

12   Lewis, "Christianity and Culture," 24.

13   C.S. Lewis, *The Abolition of Man* (New York: The Macmillan Company, 1947), 29.

14   Lewis, "Christianity and Culture," 7.

15   Clyde Kilby, ed., *A Mind Awake: An Anthology of C.S. Lewis* (New York: Harcourt, Brace, & World, 1968), 8.

16   C.S. Lewis, *The Problem of Pain* (New York: The Macmillan Company, 1962), 111.

17   Kilby, *A Mind Awake*, 211.

18   Ibid., 94.

19   C.S. Lewis, An Experiment in Criticism (Cambridge: Cambridge University Press, 1965), 100–101.

20   C.S. Lewis, The Four Loves, (London: Collins, Fontana Books, 1960), 58, 62.

21   Ibid., 9.

22   This is what Philip Ryken calls Lewis in "Lewis as the Patron Saint of American Evangelicalism" in *C.S. Lewis and the Church: Essays in Honor of Walter Hooper*, ed. Judith Wolfe and Brendan N. Wolfe (London: T&T Clark, 2011), 174–186. But Ryken is not among those who would object to correcting Lewis's doctrine in public.

23   "Lewis, as we have seen in the scope of this study, stands in sharp contrast to evangelical fundamentalism. His example proves that one can be a dedicated evangelical, accept the full authority of Scripture, yet disbelieve in inerrancy." Michael J. Christensen, *C.S. Lewis on Scripture* (Waco, Texas: Word Books, 1979), 91. Lewis speaks of the predictions of the Second Coming in one generation as

"error" in "The World's Last Night" in *C.S. Lewis: Essay Collection and Other Short Pieces* (London: Harper Collins, 2000), 45.

24 "The process whereby 'Faith and Works' became a stock gag in the commercial theater is characteristic of that whole tragic farce which we call the history of the Reformation. The theological questions really at issue have no significance except on a certain level, a high-level, of the spiritual life; they could have been fruitfully debated only between mature and saintly disputants in close privacy and at boundless leisure. Under those conditions formulae might possibly have been found which did justice to the Protestant ... assertions without compromising other elements of the Christian faith. In fact, however, these questions were raised at a moment when they immediately became embittered and entangled with a whole complex of matters theologically irrelevant, and therefore attracted the fatal attention both of government and the mob. When once this has happened, Europe's chance to come through unscathed was lost." C.S. Lewis, *English Literature in the Sixteenth Century, Excluding Drama* (Oxford: Oxford University Press, 1953), 37.

25 C.S. Lewis, *Letters of C.S. Lewis*, ed. W.H. Lewis and Walter Hooper (New York: Harcourt Brace Jovanovich, 1966), 223, 230.

26 After visiting Greece with his dying wife, he wrote, "At Daphne it was hard not to pray to Apollo the

Healer. But somehow one didn't feel it would have been very wrong—would only have been addressing Christ sub specie Apollinis." *Letters of C.S. Lewis*, ed. W. H. Lewis and Walter Hooper, revised edition (New York: Harcourt Brace Jovanovich, 1993), 468. In this way of talking about possibly praying to Christ through Apollo, he is doing what he told a mother in a letter about her son who feared he loved Aslan more than Jesus: "But Laurence can't really love Aslan more than Jesus, even if he feels that's what he's doing. For the things he loves Aslan for doing or saying are simply the things Jesus really did and said. So that when Laurence thinks he is loving Aslan, he is really loving Jesus: and perhaps loving him more than he ever did before." C.S. Lewis, *Letters to Children*, ed. Lyle W. Dorsett and Marjorie Lamp Mead (New York: Macmillian, 1985), p. 57. Most familiar is the conversion of Emeth (Hebrew for "faithful" or "true"), the sincere seeker in another religion. C.S. Lewis, *The Last Battle* (New York: The Macmillan Company, 1957), 155–157.

27 C.S. Lewis, *The Problem of Pain* (New York: The Macmillan Company, 1962), 26–88. But Lewis's view is not simple or completely transparent. He could say, "You will certainly carry out God's purpose, however you act, but it makes a difference to you whether you serve like Judas or like John." *Problem of Pain*, p. 111. And one wonders if by "free will" Lewis sometimes only means "voluntary" rather than "having ultimate self-determination." For

example, he writes, "After all, when we are most free, it is only with freedom God has given us; and when our will is most influenced by Grace, it is still *our will*. And if what our will does is not voluntary, and if 'voluntary' does not mean 'free', what are we talking about?" *Letters of C.S. Lewis*, 1966, p. 246. And perhaps most significantly, after saying that a fallen soul "could still turn back to God," he adds this footnote: "Theologians will note that I am not here intending to make any contribution to the Pelagian-Augustinian controversy. I mean only that such a return to God was not, even now, an impossibility. Where the initiative lies in any instance of such return is a question on which I am saying nothing." *The Problem of Pain*, 83.

28   To a Roman Catholic he wrote in 1941, "Yes—I think I gave the impression of going further than I intended, in saying that all theories of the Atonement were 'to be rejected if we don't find them helpful.' What I meant was 'need not be used'—a very different thing. Is there, on your view, a real difference here: that the Divinity of Our Lord *has to be* believed whether you find it helpful or a 'scandal' (otherwise you're not a Christian at all) but the Anselmic theory of Atonement is not in that position. Would you admit that a man was a Christian (and could be a member of your church) who said 'I believe that Christ's death redeemed man from sin, but I can make nothing of the theories as to *how*'? You see, what I wanted to do in these talks was

simply to give what is common to us all, and I've
been trying to get a *nihil obstat* from friends in vari-
ous communions. ... It therefore doesn't much matter how you think of my own theory, because that
is advanced only as my own." *Letters of C.S. Lewis*,
1966, 197–198.

29   "For Lewis the doctrines were always absolutely
necessary as maps toward one's true destination—
they should never be the goal of the Christian life."
Alan Jacobs, *The Narnian: The Life and Imagination of C.S. Lewis* (New York: HarperOne, 2006),
293.

30   C.S. Lewis, *The Weight of Glory and Other Addresses* (Grand Rapids: Eerdmans, 1965), 1–2.

31   Pascal, *Pensees*, 113.

32   C.S. Lewis, *Reflections on the Psalms* (New York:
Harcourt, Brace & World, 1958), 94–95.

33   Augustine, *Confessions*, 181 (IX.1), emphasis added.

34   John Calvin, *The Institutes of the Christian Religion*,
ed. John T. McNeill (Philadelphia: Westminster
Press, 1960), 192–193 (I.15.6).

35   Thomas Watson, *Body of Divinity* (1692; repr.
Grand Rapids: Baker, 1979), 10.

36   Quoted from an unpublished sermon, "Sacrament
Sermon on Canticles 5:1" (circa 1729), edited ver-
sion by Kenneth Minkema in association with *The
Works of Jonathan Edwards*, Yale University.

37   Jonathan Edwards, "The Spiritual Blessings of the Gospel Represented by a Feast," in *The Works of Jonathan Edwards*, vol. 17, *Sermons and Discourses, 1723–1729*, ed. Kenneth P. Minkema (New Haven, Conn.: Yale University Press, 1996), 286.

38   Charles Hodge, "The Excellency of the Knowledge of Christ Jesus Our Lord," in *Princeton Sermons: Outlines of Discourses, Doctrinal and Practical* (London: Thomas Nelson and Sons, Paternoster Row, 1870), 214.

39   Geerhardus Vos, *The Pauline Eschatology* (1930; repr. Grand Rapids: Eerdmans, 1966), 71, emphasis added.

40   C.S. Lewis, *Letters to Malcolm Chiefly on Prayer* (New York: Harcourt Brace Jovanovich, 1963), 89–90.

41   This is an excerpt from a letter to "Joan," a child who wrote him on July 18, 1957, in *C.S. Lewis: Letters to Children*, ed. Lyle W. Dorsett and Marjorie Lamp Mead (New York: Simon & Schuster, 1995), 276.

42   C.S. Lewis, *Reflections on the Psalms* (New York: Harcourt, Brace & World, 1958), 93–5.

43   C.S. Lewis, *Surprised by Joy* (New York: Harcourt, Brace and World, 1955), 18.

44   Jeremy Taylor, quoted in C.S. Lewis, *George MacDonald: An Anthology* (London: Geoffrey Bles, 1946), 19.

45 C.S. Lewis, *The Weight of Glory and Other Address-es* (Grand Rapids: Eerdmans, 1965), 2.

46 Some philosophers of science, like Michael Ruse, *say* they believe morality is no more than a biologi-cal survival development, but I doubt that they live that way. Ruse writes, "The position of the modern evolutionist is that … morality is a biological adapta-tion no less than are hands and feet and teeth. Con-sidered as a rationally justifiable set of claims about an objective something, ethics is illusory. I appre-ciate that when somebody says 'Love thy neighbor as thyself,' they think they are referring above and beyond themselves. Nevertheless, such reference is truly without foundation. Morality is just an aid to survival and reproduction … and any deeper mean-ing is illusory." Michael Ruse, "Evolutionary Theo-ry and Christian Ethics," in *The Darwinian Para-digm* (London: Routledge, 1989), 262–269.

47 C.S. Lewis, "Transposition," in *The Weight of Glo-ry and Other Addresses* (Grand Rapids: Eerdmans, 1949), 26. "I suspect that, save by God's direct mir-acle, spiritual experience can never abide introspec-tion. If even our emotions will not do so, (since the attempt to find out what we are now feeling yields nothing more than a physical sensation) much less will the operations of the Holy Ghost. The attempt to discover by introspective analysis our own spir-itual condition is to me a horrible thing which reveals, at best, not the secrets of God's spirit and ours, but their transposition in intellect, emotion and imagination, and which at worst may be the quickest road to presumption or despair."

48   Lewis, "Transposition," 24.

49   Ibid., 28.

50   C.S. Lewis, "Meditation in a Toolshed," in *God in the Dock* (Grand Rapids: Eerdmans, 1970), 212.

51   The exact quote is, "The difference between the almost right word and the right word is really a large matter—it's the difference between the lightning bug and the lightning." It is taken from a letter from Mark Twain to George Bainton (October 15, 1888), first printed in *The Art of Authorship: Literary Reminiscences, Methods of Work, and Advice to Young Beginners, Personally Contributed by Leading Authors of the Day*, comp. and ed. George Bainton (New York: D. Appleton and Company, 1890), 85–88.

52   Richard Foster, "A Pastoral Letter from Richard Foster" in the November 1996 issue of Heart to Heart, a publication of Foster's ministry, *Renovaré*, 1–3.

53   "One minute would see Miss D. compressed, clenched, and blocked, or jerking, ticcing, and jabbering—like a sort of human bomb; the next, with the sound of music from a wireless or a gramophone, the complete disappearance of all these obstructive-explosive phenomena and their replacement by a blissful ease and flow of movement as Miss D.,

suddenly freed of her automatisms, smilingly 'conducted' the music, or rose and danced to it." Quoted from Oliver Sachs, *Awakenings*, in Robert Jourdain, *Music, the Brain, and Ecstasy: How Music Captures Our Imagination* (New York: William Morrow and Company, 1997), 301.

54   Numerous Internet sites discuss this research. E.g., http://www.epub.org.br/cm/n15/mente/musica.html.

55   I am aware that so much more could be said about the possibilities and perils of music in the spiritual life. I would like to recommend that you pursue this further in Harold M. Best, *Music Through the Eyes of Faith* (San Francisco: HarperCollins, 1993). This is the most helpful and provocative book I know of on the spiritual function of music.

56   I do not recall the source for this quote. It is simply there in my memorabilia, and may have been a letter or recollection from class.

57   G.K. Chesterton, Orthodoxy (1924; repr. Garden City, N.Y.: Image Books, 1959), 12.

58   Ibid., 20–21.

59   Ibid., 54.

60   Ibid., 55.

61   Ibid., 60.

62   The quote is from Bertrand Russell, *The*

Autobiography of Bertrand Russell, 3 vols. (London: George Allen and Unwin, 1968), 2:159.

63 What he means by abstracting is taking concrete examples and reducing them to the abstraction of generalities. For example, dealing in concrete specifics means seeing and savoring a particular oak tree in your front yard where you climbed as a child and where you carved your initials when you fell in love. But dealing in abstractions means lumping this tree into a category and speaking abstractly of all oak trees.

64 The quote comes from the prefatory verse to Lewis Carroll's *Through the Looking Glass*.

65 Darwin gave this advice out of great regret looking back over his life. Near the end of his life, in the autobiography that he wrote for his children, Darwin said, "Up to the age of 30 or beyond it, poetry of many kinds ... gave me great pleasure, and even as a schoolboy I took intense delight in Shakespeare. ... Formerly pictures gave me considerable, and music very great, delight. But now for many years I cannot endure to read a line of poetry: I have tried to read Shakespeare, and found it so intolerably dull that it nauseated me. I have also almost lost any taste for pictures or music. ... I retain some taste for fine scenery, but it does not cause me the exquisite delight which it formerly did. ... My mind seems to have become a kind of machine for grinding general laws out of large collections of facts, but why this should have caused the atrophy of that part of the brain alone, on which the higher tastes depend, I cannot conceive. ... The loss of these tastes is a loss of happiness, and may possibly be injurious to the intellect, and more probably to the moral character, by enfeebling the emotional part of our nature." Cited in Virginia Stem Owens, "Seeing Christianity in Red and Green as Well as Black and White," *Christianity Today* 2 (September 2, 1983), 38.

66   Jonathan Edwards, "God Glorified in the Work of Redemption, by the Greatness of Man's Dependence upon Him, in the Whole of It (1731)" (sermon on 1 Corinthians 1:29–31), in *The Sermons of Jonathan Edwards: A Reader*, ed. Wilson H. Kimnach, Kenneth Minkema, and Douglas A. Sweeney (New Haven, Conn.: Yale University Press, 1999), 75.

67   Jonathan Edwards, "Miscellanies" no. 95, in *The Works of Jonathan Edwards*, vol. 13, The "Miscellanies," a-500, ed. Thomas Schafer (New Haven, Conn.: Yale University Press, 1994), 263, emphasis added.

68   Sereno E. Dwight, "Memoirs of Jonathan Edwards," in *The Works of Jonathan Edwards*, ed. Edward Hickman (1834; repr. Edinburgh: Banner of Truth, 1974), 1:xxxviii.

69   Ibid., xxxv.

70   Ibid., xxi.

71 For guidance from a biblical perspective, see Elyse Fitzpatrick, *Love to Eat, Hate to Eat: Breaking the Bondage of Destructive Eating Habits* (Eugene, Ore.: Harvest House, 1999).

72 http://www.endovascular.net/EXERCIZE.html. Accessed 5-26-04.

73 Charles Haddon Spurgeon, *Lectures to My Students* (1875, 1877; repr. Grand Rapids: Zondervan, 1972), 160.

74 Eric W. Hayden, *Highlights in the Life of C. H. Spurgeon* (Pasadena, Tex.: Pilgrim Publications, 1990), 103.

75 Spurgeon, *Lectures to My Students*, 161.

76 Ibid., 158.

77 Ibid., 312.

78 Quoted from Clyde Kilby, ed., *The Four Loves* in *A Mind Awake: An Anthology of C.S. Lewis* (New York: Harcourt, Brace & World, 1968), 85.

79 Quoted from *The Problem of Pain*, in Ibid., 80.